08/0037 D

HALTON

Rising, Wild, and Beckoning

Acknowledgements

INDIVIDUALS	PHOTOGRAPHERS	ORGANIZATIONS	FOUNDATION DIRECTORS
Rick Archbold	Richard Armstrong	Bronte Creek Provincial Park	Janet K. Mitchell, Chair
Brenda Axon	Jack Arno	Bruce Trail Association	Ken Moore, Vice Chair
Dr. Roberta Bondar	Brenda Axon	Burlington Arts Centre	Jack Arno
Dave Brewer	Birgit Bateman	Burlington Fine Arts Association	Barry Slater
Chris Burnett	Robert Bateman	City of Burlington	Roy Wilson
Tom Chudleigh	Sandy Bell	Conservation Lands of Ontario	Theresa Magure-Garber
Lois Crawford	Rob Boak	Conservation Ontario	Gary Hutton
Sheila Creighton	Roberta Bondar	Credit Valley Conservation Foundation	Anthony H. Beale
David Crombie	Sheilah Creighton	Escarpment Country Tourism	Ken Brandson
Brian Darcy	Alan Ernst	Esquesing Historical Society	William E. French
Alan Day	Gary Fliss	Federation of Ontario Naturalists	Don C. Ford
John Denison	Geoff Grenville	Halton Region Conservation Authority	John P. Ford
Paul Duff	Halton Region Conservation	Halton Region Museum	Dick M. Haas
Darlene Duncan	Authority	Milton Chamber of Commerce	Sarah B. Lowe
Dr. William D. Finlayson	Susan Hanson	Niagara Escarpment Commission	Cindy Lunau
Ann Guthrie	Neil Hester	Oakville Public Library	Bill Robinson
Murray Harris	Malcom Hopkinson	Ontario Agricultural Museum	James Snow
Paul Heersink	Gary Hutton	Regional Municipality of Halton	Brian Penman
Gayle Hutchings	Pat Keough	Royal Botanical Gardens	Alan Bennett
Pat Keough	Rosemarie Keough	The Grand River Foundation	George Grummett
Rosemarie Keough	Ron Kindt	Town of Flamborough	Anne Ptolemy
Marlaine Koehler	Lori Labatt	Town of Halton Hills	Robert Bateman
Dr. Doug Larson	Jeff Marko	Town of Milton	Birgit Bateman
Diane Leblovic	Robert McCaw	Town of Oakville	G. Allan Burton
Margaret Lott	Janice McDermott	University of Guelph	Ninalee Craig
Ray Lowes	Maggie Mills	Waterdown-East Flamborough Heritage Society	
Dr. Jock McAndrews	Scott Robertson	Waterfront Regeneration Trust	
Jeff McColl	Philip Schmidt		
Dave and Margie Moore	Rob Stimpson		
Brian Penman	University of Guelph		
Dorothy Turcotte	Simon Wilson		
E. Robert Ross	Gord Wood		
Dr. John Todd	WorldSat International Inc.		
Debra Vanderwal	Mark Zelinski		
Janet Wilson			

THE CONSERVATION LANDS OF ONTARIO

HALTON

Rising, Wild, and Beckoning

CONSERVATION HALTON FOUNDATION

FOREWORD BY ROBERT BATEMAN • TEXT BY ANN GUTHRIE

DEDICATION

*This book is dedicated to
Douglas G. Cockburn and Marguerite Gray,
Delhi, Ontario
in appreciation of exemplary support to conservation
at the Mountsberg Conservation Area.*

BOOK COMMITTEE CHAIR - Barry Slater
PROJECT CO-ORDINATOR AND EDITOR - Gary Hutton
TEXT - Ann Guthrie, Guelph
WATERSHED MAPS - Chismar Mapping Services Inc., Uxbridge
TRAIL MAPS - Paperglyphs, Lindsay
Design - Gillian Stead, The Boston Mills Press
Editing - The Boston Mills Press

Halton Region Conservation Foundation
2596 Britannia Road West
R.R. #2 Milton, Ontario
L9T 2X6
(905) 336-1158 or FAX (905) 336-7014
www.hrca.on.ca

CANADIAN CATALOGUING IN PUBLICATION DATA

Main entry under title:

Halton: rising, wild and beckoning

ISBN 1-55046-286-3

1. Halton (Ont.)-Guidebooks. 2. Rivers-Ontario-Halton-Guidebooks.
3. Natural history-Ontario-Halton-Guidebooks. 4. Halton (Ont.)-
Pictorial works. I. Conservation Halton Foundation.

FC3095.H345A3 1998   917'13'533044   C98-931717-X
F1059.H28H35 1998

Copyright © 1998 Halton Conservation Foundation

Produced by the Boston Mills Press
132 Main Street
Erin, Ontario
Canada N0B 1T0
(519) 833-2407

Printed in Hong Kong by
Book Art Inc., Toronto

Wetland artistry at the Harrison Resource Management Area, Campbellville. NEIL HESTER

SPONSORS

OAKVILLE
ONTARIO

Halton: Rising, Wild, and Beckoning is a celebration of the rich and abundant conservation lands of the Halton watershed. The Halton Region Conservation Foundation gratefully acknowledges the sponsors who supported the production of this book.

 **FRIENDS** *of the* **ENVIRONMENT** *Foundation*

Supported by Canada Trust and Its Customers   BURLINGTON, OAKVILLE AND MILTON CHAPTERS

 **CLUBLINK CORPORATION**    GEORGETOWN GOLF CLUB    BLUE SPRINGS GOLF CLUB   GREYSTONE GOLF·CLUB   RATTLESNAKE POINT GOLF CLUB

 Rodger Recruiting Inc.

O A K V I L L E

 LEADING BY BUILDING VALUE FOR YOU   Dufferin Aggregates, a Division of St. Lawrence Cement Inc., is a leading supplier of high quality crushed stone, sand and gravel to the Greater Toronto area. The company has a commitment to resource stewardship through the design of its operations, rehabilitation and environmental monitoring. Dufferin's Milton quarry in the Region of Halton is being rehabilitated to a naturalized area with lakes, cliffs amd wetlands, designed to fit in with the natural beauty of the surrounding Niagara Escarpment. The company is pleased to support the work of the Conservation Foundation.

 **Milton Limestone** Division of Lac Properties Inc.   *Together, we can achieve our common goals for sound management, conservation and renewed public use of our natural resources.*

  **CENTRAL CLEANING BEAM SYSTEMS** Oakville • Cambridge    *The Way To Go!* **Bruce Hood Travel** AMERICAN EXPRESS *Professional Travel & Cruise Officials* Milton • Halton Hills • Oakville   **SHERMAN** ▪ **SAND & GRAVEL LIMITED** ▪ *Milton*

Bell Canada • Chrismar Mapping Services Inc., Uxbridge • Ninalee Craig, Burlington • Kathy and Tom Fraser, Halton Hills • Ann Guthrie, Guelph • Hogarth Printing Co. Ltd., Mississauga • Janet and Robert Mitchell, Oakville • Moore Resources Systems Ltd., Campbellville • The Rotary Club of Oakville • Philip Analytical Services Corp., Burlington • Ridley Windows and Doors, Campbellville • James and Barbara Snow, Hornby • Svedas, Koyanagi Architects Inc., Burlington

Ruth Anderson, Campbellville, In Memory of Hugh J. Anderson • Anthony and Anne Beale, Milton • Allan Burton, Burlington • APAO, Mississauga • Blue Circle Aggregates Canada, Mississauga • Curwood Packaging, Halton Hills • Theresa Maguire-Garber, Stoney Creek, In memory of John A. Maguire Sr. • Dick M. Haas, Brampton, In memory of David Haas Halton Crushed Stone Limited, Milton • James Dick Construction, Bolton • Laidlaw Inc., Burlington • Nelson Aggregates Co., Burlington • Nicolas and Diane Leblovic, Burlington Lura Consulting, Toronto • Moss, Lawson Company Limited, Toronto • Northrop Grumman, Burlington • Old is Beautiful Antiques, Moffat • Procor Ltd., Oakville • Doug and Anne Ptolemy, Milton • Barry Slater, Mississauga • Stelco Inc., Hilton Works, Hamilton • Sunoco Inc., Campbellville • Swift Sure Group, Oakville • Terra Green Houses, Waterdown The Hamilton Hospitals Assessment Centre, In memory of Nancy French • WorldSat International Inc., Mississauga

Dorothy Brown, Milton • Andrew Bryant, Burlington • Dighem, A Division of C.G.G. Canada, Mississauga • Dr. and Mrs. H.G. Downie, Cambridge • Wilson Eedy, Moffat • Mr. and Mrs. R. Elliott, Carlisle Louise Frankow, Georgetown • Mrs. Brock Harris, Burlington • Mr. and Mrs. K.O. Horwood, Oakville • Gary, Terrie and Cameron Hutton • J. Ross Knechtel, Guelph • Joan Little, Burlington Log House Craft Gallery, Campbellville • Long Lane Orchards, Milton • Madison Press Books, Toronto • Allan M. Masson, Oakville • Nadia and Sylvia McCormick, Campbellville James Morton, Burlington • Dianne Taylor, Campbellville Aline Tso, Burlington • Carter B. Wasilka, Hillsburgh • Derrick and Jean Williams, Mississauga

HILTON FALLS CONSERVATION AREA, MILTON.   PHILIP SCHMIDT

Hilton Falls Conservation Area, Milton.
PHILIP SCHMIDT

CONTENTS

FOREWORD by Robert Bateman   9

INTRODUCTION: Watching Birds in Grandpa's Woods   11

CHAPTER 1   About the Watershed: A Natural History   13

CHAPTER 2   Halton's First People: 21
              Secrets of Crawford Lake

CHAPTER 3   Early Pioneers: Sugaring Off at Mountsberg   29

CHAPTER 4   Halton's Backbone: 37
              The Niagara Escarpment

CHAPTER 5   Hidden Treasures of Bronte Creek   45

CHAPTER 6   The Sixteen Mile Creek Mystery Tour   53

CHAPTER 7   Chasing Waterfalls   61
              on Halton Conservation Lands

CHAPTER 8   Legendary Promontories: 69
              Kelso and Rattlesnake Point

CHAPTER 9   Limestone Legacy and Scenic Links: 77
              Exploring Halton Hills

CHAPTER 10   Country Roads and Rural Roots: 85
              Exploring Milton

CHAPTER 11   Secret Gardens and Natural Spaces: 93
              Exploring Oakville

CHAPTER 12   Mount Nemo Magic and Inspiring Waterways: 101
              Exploring Burlington

CHAPTER 13   Along the Shore of Lake Ontario: 109
              The Waterfront Trail

CHAPTER 14   Artisans of the Natural Landscape   117

CHAPTER 15   Lands for Learning and Raptor Rapture   125

CHAPTER 16   Rising, Wild and Protected: 133
              Conservation Halton

CONCLUSION by Pat and Rosemarie Keough   141

AFTERWORD   143

RICH FARMLANDS SURROUND THE NIAGARA ESCARPMENT IN HALTON WATERSHED, BURLINGTON. NEIL HESTER

FOREWORD

All my life I dreamed of living in the country, close to nature but near enough to an urban centre so that I could partake of museums, concerts and theatre. By my late twenties, I was starting to transform my dreams into plans. When I returned from an around-the-world Landrover trip in 1958, I took a job at Nelson High School in Burlington. My main motive in doing this was the proximity of the Niagara Escarpment and the traditional rural countryside of the Halton watershed. Within a week or two of school opening in September, I set forth with a topographic map to find the future site of my "dream home." I wanted a woods, a stream and a view, in that order, and was lucky enough to find an available lot with a beautiful view of Rattlesnake Point. I also fell in love with the Halton watershed.

The Halton watershed has wildness without remoteness. It can be rugged and secluded, yet accessible. In the 1950s it had, and to a large extent still has, a subtle blend of human heritage and nature. Our forebearers created family farms, but because of the escarpment and the creek valleys, they had to work around nature and leave generous bits more or less intact. Some of the most elegant and charming parts of the world are those areas where traditional human settlement and activities have a gentle

Young Robert Bateman in a Halton meadow. BIRGIT BATEMAN

and compatible interface with nature. Large sections of the Halton watershed remain this way, but of course this precious blend is being threatened by the "instant pudding" development that has been bulldozing its way across North America for several decades.

I have visited majestic wilderness areas and massive urban centres. Of course, I prefer the former, but both are awesome. Overwhelming size and spectacle are fine, but as a steady diet, I like the human scale of the traditional parts of Halton. And in a world that is increasingly going "global," human scale is becoming more and more rare and valuable. Many of the most meaningful aspects of the Halton watershed are measured by the square meter — the detail of a Victorian house, an old pine barn timber, the bark of a beech tree or roadside meadow flowers.

You need to be an intimate viewer, and this is the way to enjoy this book — through the creative eyes of a number of artists with cameras, who also love the Halton watershed.

Robert Bateman,
Robert Bateman,
Saltspring Island, British Columbia

Watching birds at Rattlesnake Point Conservation Area, Milton. Neil Hester

INTRODUCTION
Watching Birds in Grandpa's Woods

In days gone by, to experience the natural world you need go no further than a nearby stream or the woods at Grandpa's farm. Today that experience is still available in the Halton watershed. Community leaders with the foresight to recognize the intrinsic value and exquisite beauty of conservation lands and parks have preserved them.

Halton: Rising, Wild and Beckoning is a guide to one of the most charming places in Ontario. Halton has a subtle blend of human and natural history; this book beckons you to look for and explore the natural and cultural treasures of Halton's vibrant communities and wondrous conservation lands.

The late Roger Tory Peterson, famous artist and author of the *Peterson Field Guide to Birds*, once said, "Birds are a visual treat that reaffirms the joy and goodness of living. Because birds fly and are not rooted to the earth, they are the most elegant expression of life."

Just like a field guide, this book presents readers with a menu of natural outdoor experiences, complete with maps and guideposts on how to get there. In each chapter, "nature calls" with featured wildlife and their unmistakable voices.

The book's spectacular photographs show the diversity and variety of landscapes in the Halton watershed. As if looking through binoculars, you can see on these pages the power of nature's beauty, where whispering streams become thundering waterfalls, narrow tree-lined paths end at panoramic vistas and distant migrating birds can be seen close up.

An Indigo Bunting sings in a spring forest.
ROBERT MCCAW

From just about anywhere in the watershed, you can see turkey vultures soaring over the landscape. These magnificent birds of prey symbolize the "wild" aspects of Halton's abundant conservation lands.

The watershed is a haven for artists and craftspeople who are inspired by the natural landscape. Scientists are attracted to the area because of the wealth of knowledge to be gleaned from the unique environment. From archaeological sites and a rare meromictic lake to the ancient cedars of Ontario's oldest-growth forest, the area has a treasure trove of fascinating features.

Most of all, the Halton watershed is a great place for people to have fun and relax. From rock climbing and skiing to hiking and birdwatching, the recreational opportunities are almost endless. You can also enjoy antique and craft shops, pick-your-own farms, great bed-and-breakfast spots, historic churches and scenic drives.

Read and enjoy this book as if you were watching birds in Grandpa's woods. Look, listen and search for all that is rising, wild and beckoning in the Halton watershed. You won't be disappointed.

Gary Hutton,
editor, *Halton: Rising, Wild and Beckoning*

A SATELLITE IMAGE OF THE HALTON WATERSHED AS TAKEN BY THE LANDSAT SATELLITE FROM 705 KILOMETRES ABOVE THE EARTH. WORLDSAT INC.

1

ABOUT THE WATERSHED: A Natural History

Although I cared deeply about the environment before I flew in space, I became passionate about it during my flight. When I was in space, looking down on our magnificent blue-and-green planet Earth and I couldn't see the borders between the countries, I realized how fragile the world is and how truly unique Canada is. This country, with its fresh water, soil, atmosphere and access to various types of climate within its own range of geography, may well be the saving grace for the whole planet. After space flight everything on the planet seems very delicate, except for the rocks and the crust of the earth. The life forms that live upon it are intricate and rely on each other. We cannot deny the progress and rapid change that affect all living things that share the same soil, air and water, but we must let them breathe and learn how to let them live. Failure to do so strips us of any possibility of survival. Fortunately, in this country, wise people have taken steps to understand, cherish and preserve these intricate life forms through dedicated programs. The Halton watershed, with its abundant conservation lands, has excellent conservation programs that protect the region's vulnerable natural areas. The watershed includes the world-renowned Niagara Escarpment, Carolinian forests, Lake Ontario shoreline, creeks, valleys and rich wetlands. Conservation programs such as the restoration of Cootes Paradise and the rehabilitation of birds of prey at the Mountsberg Conservation Area show that it is possible to make conservation and preservation an integral part of urban growth, even in Canada's most populated areas.

DR. ROBERTA BONDAR, ASTRONAUT, PHYSICIAN, SCIENTIST AND NATURE PHOTOGRAPHER

Photographs of Earth taken from space allow us to see our planet as a whole, interconnected system, undivided by arbitrary social and political boundaries. From space, borders become meaningless. Closer to home, a watershed is a similar interrelated system, connecting land and water. The natural flow of rivers and creeks is a metaphor for such a holistic understanding of the environment, as natural watercourses cannot be confined to human boundaries. Instead, rivers unite nature and humans within their watersheds. Everything is connected.

The Halton watershed is located in the "Golden Horseshoe," the most densely populated area of Canada. As the creeks of the watershed flow from their headwaters to Lake Ontario, they pass through large tracts of forest, agricultural lands and urban development, connecting human settlement and wildlife habitat. A watershed, simply defined, is the land drained by a stream or watercourse. A

Bloodroot leaves unfurl in early spring.
ROBERTA BONDAR

watershed approach to environmental planning is more profound, as it speaks of the interconnections between every organism within an ecosystem. Ontario's conservation authorities are pioneers in watershed planning. The Halton Region Conservation Authority was established in 1963 with the amalgamation of Sixteen Mile Creek and Twelve Mile Creek Conservation Authorities. At that time, the watershed boundary was enlarged to include the drainage basins of Grindstone and Joshua's Creeks. Today the Halton watershed includes 1,046 square kilometres of land, drained by three major watercourses — Grindstone, Bronte and Sixteen Mile Creeks — and fourteen smaller streams. The Halton watershed includes portions of the regional municipalities of Halton, Hamilton-Wentworth, and Peel, and the County of Wellington.

The Niagara Escarpment, with its picturesque bluffs, deep valleys, scenic waterfalls, and rugged hills, is the dominant landform in the Halton watershed. The escarpment was formed 450 million years ago when a shallow tropical sea covered vast portions of Ontario and Michigan. Over the succeeding millions of years, glacial and other erosion carved the layers of sandstone, shale and limestone into dramatic cliffs and craggy slopes. Mount Nemo and Rattlesnake Point are examples of the numerous sites of geological significance in the watershed.

The Niagara Escarpment divides the Halton watershed, creating distinctive features above and below the escarpment. Above the escarpment, glaciers shaped the lands, leaving behind deposits of sand and gravel known as the Waterdown Moraine, Flamborough Plain and Horseshoe Moraine. These are important recharging areas for groundwater and augment low flows in Bronte, Grindstone and Sixteen Mile Creeks.

In the land above the escarpment, wetlands abound. The Halton watershed contains twelve wetlands considered provincially significant, including the Hayesland, Beverly and Badenoch–Moffat Swamps. These wetland complexes contain various habitats for uncommon birds, amphibians and reptiles. Wetlands are critical to river systems, as they retain floodwaters, filter sediment and pollutants to improve water quality, and provide rich and diverse habitats for many species of flora and fauna. The ecological significance of wetlands, however, has not always been understood. Pioneers regarded swamps as wastelands and drained them to create farmland. The tide is turning again as conservation organizations strive to restore these valuable natural environments.

As the creeks descend the escarpment slope, they pass through the Peel Plain at its base. Bronte and Sixteen Mile Creeks have carved deep valleys into the clay soil that characterizes the Peel Plain. The land then begins to flatten out as the creeks reach the Iroquois Plain that surrounds the Lake Ontario shoreline and was once part of glacial Lake Iroquois. The Royal Botanical Gardens, in the lower portion of Grindstone Creek watershed, protect portions of this vulnerable ecosystem. With 1,094 hectares of untamed and cultivated landscapes, the internationally renowned site is a paradise in Canada's industrial heartland.

The Lake Ontario waterfront is a critical part of the Halton watershed with over 36 kilometres of shoreline. Regeneration of the Lake Ontario waterfront has become a priority for concerned citizens and public agencies. Since the 1980s, Burlington, Oakville and the Halton Region Conservation Authority have had a renewed commitment to the waterfront, including the development of a shoreline management plan for conservation.

The varied topography and geological features of the Halton watershed support a diversity of habitats for wildlife. The Niagara Escarpment is a vital corridor for flora and fauna. Habitats with cliff face, talus slope, crevices, and tableland forests support specialized plant species. There is an abundance of ferns — of the 120 species located in North America, 40 varieties can be found in the Halton area. During spring, woodland wildflowers, such as wild leek, hepatica, blue cohosh and dogtooth violet, herald a new cycle of growth.

About twenty-five percent of the Halton watershed is covered by

Dense forest surrounds a rare meromictic lake at
Crawford Lake Conservation Area, Milton. Geoff Grenville

BRONTE CREEK GORGE, OAKVILLE. GEOFF GRENVILLE

forest, which is quite high for its Golden Horseshoe location. The watershed is also a transition zone between two forest communities: the Carolinian Forest Zone and the Great Lakes–St. Lawrence Forest Region. The Carolinian Forest Zone, which includes the area along the shoreline of Lake Erie and portions of Lake Ontario, is the richest vegetation zone in Canada. In this relatively mild climate, species normally found only in more southern areas reach the northern limit of their range. Unfortunately, most of the Carolinian forest has vanished under the plow, axe and bulldozer, and only ten percent of the original forest remains. Within these scattered remnants are the greatest diversity of species in any Canadian forest zone, including fifty percent of Ontario's rare, threatened or endangered plants and animals. Some of these special habitats, such as Sassafras Woods in the Grindstone Creek watershed, have been designated as Carolinian Canada sites. Nationally and provincially rare Carolinian species found in the Halton watershed include red mulberry, pignut hickory and yellow mandarin. Virginia opossum, cerulean warblers and orchard orioles have also been observed in the last vestiges of natural habitat in the Carolinian Forest Zone.

The conservation lands of the Halton watershed are an oasis of unspoiled wilderness and open green space. The conservation lands include more than 5,500 hectares of valleys, wetlands, Lake Ontario shoreline, forests and escarpment. The unique geological features and environmentally sensitive habitats of the conservation lands are protected in conservation areas such as Hilton Falls, Crawford Lake and Rattlesnake Point, Bronte Creek Provincial Park and Royal Botanical Gardens. On any day, in any season, nature's mysteries unravel before the curious adventurer in the wild charm of Halton's conservation lands.

Watershed Guidepost
Halton's Conservation Lands

Nature is calling in the conservation lands of Halton. The Halton watershed, located in the Golden Horseshoe of Southern Ontario, is endowed with an eclectic collection of magnificent waterfalls, spectacular cliffs, rare Carolinian flora and fauna, and green spaces along the Lake Ontario shoreline. Thousands of hectares of conservation lands protect the wild beauty of the watershed. Visitors can discover the unique features of the conservation lands by exploring Halton Region conservation areas, Royal Botanical Gardens, Halton Region agreement forests, Bronte Creek Provincial Park and parkland along the Lake Ontario waterfront.

A day trip to Halton's conservation lands presents a variety of recreational opportunities, from the adrenaline rush of downhill skiing, kayaking, rock climbing and mountain biking to the more serene pleasures of hiking, birdwatching and nature photography. Each season is a unique experience at the conservation lands. With more than 150 kilometres of nature trails, including the famous Bruce Trail and the Lake Ontario Waterfront Trail, the conservation lands are islands of tranquillity and havens for outdoor adventure.

Directions: The conservation lands of the watershed are well marked with directional signs and are easy to find. Directions to specific conservation lands are included in the guideposts that accompany each chapter of *Halton: Rising, Wild and Beckoning.*

Nature Calls - Listening Points

The natural world strikes a chord in everyone. Watching the sun rise on Lake Ontario, overlooking the lush, green countryside from atop the Niagara Escarpment, or listening to the enchanting sounds of a waterfall — all of these experiences can be found in the conservation lands of the Halton watershed. Witness the spectacular changes that take place during each season. The rhythm of nature is filled with a symphony of sounds, from the honking of migrating Canada geese to the high-pitched peeping of spring peeper frogs. The conservation lands are the best places to listen to nature's many voices.

SCOTT ROBERTSON

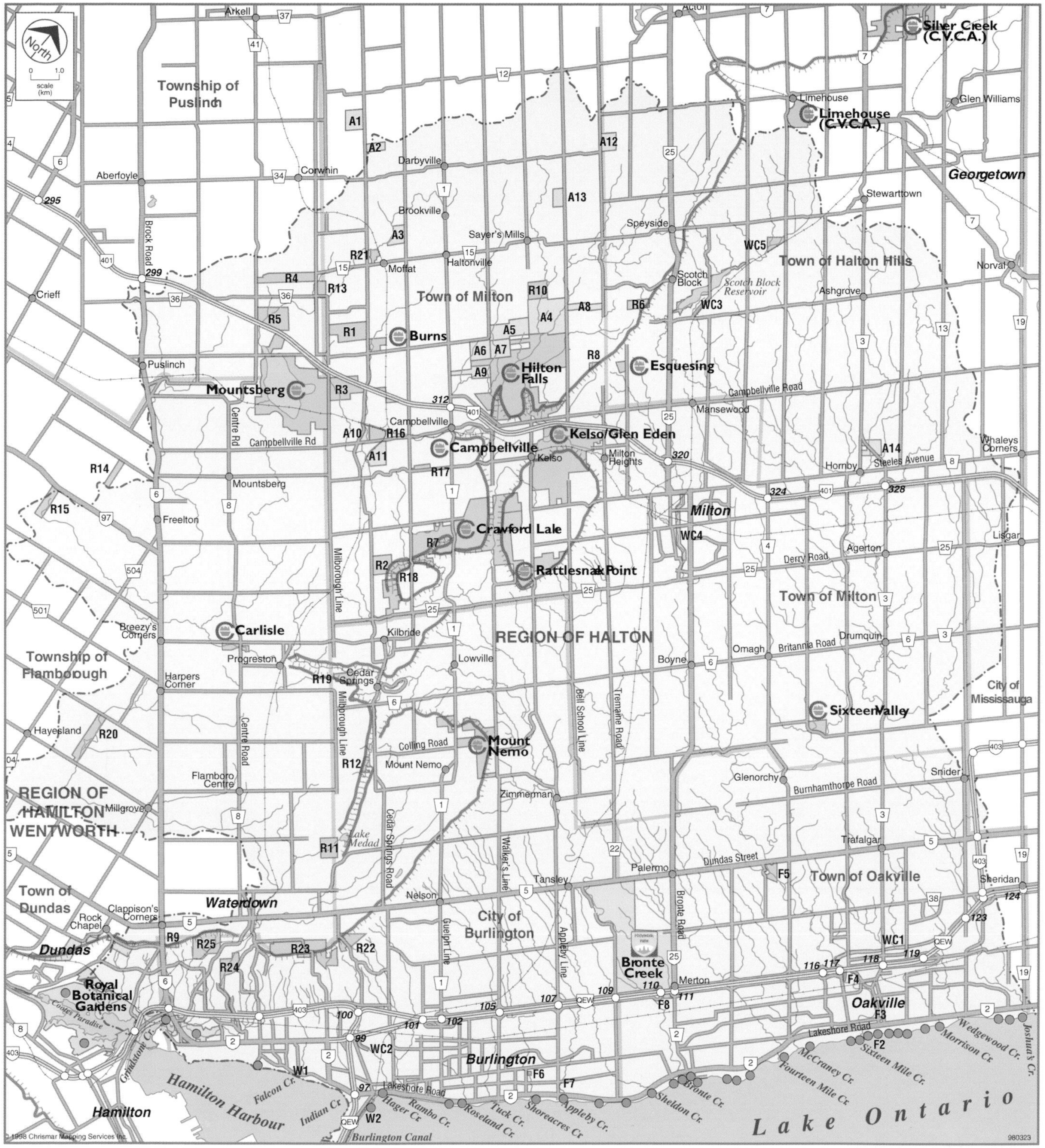

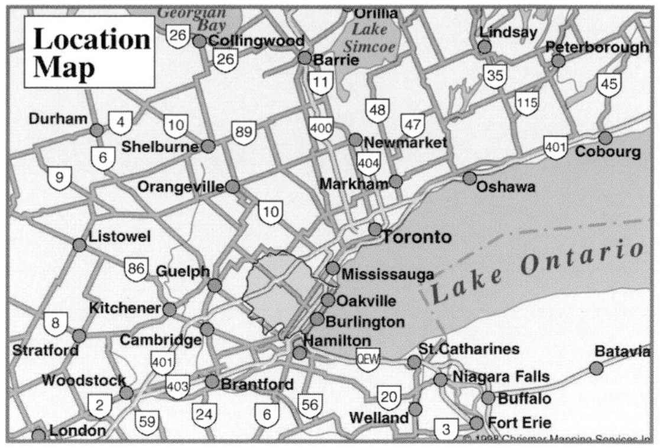

The Conservation Lands of Halton

Legend

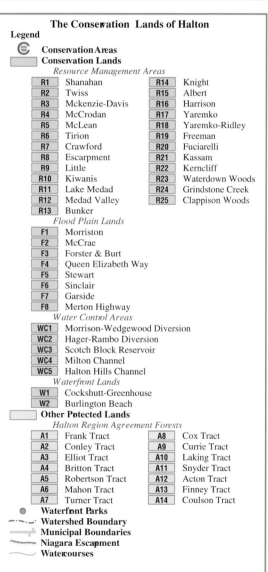

Conservation Areas

Conservation Lands

Resource Management Areas

R1	Shanahan	R14	Knight
R2	Twiss	R15	Albert
R3	Mckenzie-Davis	R16	Harrison
R4	McCrodan	R17	Yaremko
R5	McLean	R18	Yaremko-Ridley
R6	Tirion	R19	Freeman
R7	Crawford	R20	Fuciarelli
R8	Escarpment	R21	Kassam
R9	Little	R22	Kerncliff
R10	Kiwanis	R23	Waterdown Woods
R11	Lake Medad	R24	Grindstone Creek
R12	Medad Valley	R25	Clappison Woods
R13	Bunker		

Flood Plain Lands

F1	Morriston
F2	McCrae
F3	Forster & Burt
F4	Queen Elizabeth Way
F5	Stewart
F6	Sinclair
F7	Garside
F8	Merton Highway

Water Control Areas

WC1	Morrison-Wedgewood Diversion
WC2	Hager-Rambo Diversion
WC3	Scotch Block Reservoir
WC4	Milton Channel
WC5	Halton Hills Channel

Waterfront Lands

W1	Cockshutt-Greenhouse
W2	Burlington Beach

Other Protected Lands

Halton Region Agreement Forests

A1	Frank Tract	A8	Cox Tract
A2	Conley Tract	A9	Currie Tract
A3	Elliot Tract	A10	Laking Tract
A4	Britton Tract	A11	Snyder Tract
A5	Robertson Tract	A12	Acton Tract
A6	Mahon Tract	A13	Finney Tract
A7	Turner Tract	A14	Coulson Tract

Waterfront Parks

Watershed Boundary

Municipal Boundaries

Niagara Escarpment

Watercourses

GRINDSTONE CREEK, WATERDOWN. NEIL HESTER

VIEW OF MOUNT NEMO FROM RATTLESNAKE POINT CONSERVATION AREA, MILTON. NEIL HESTER

WILDFLOWERS ENCIRCLE THE RECONSTRUCTED IROQUOIAN VILLAGE AT CRAWFORD LAKE CONSERVATION AREA, MILTON. ROB STIMPSON

2

HALTON'S FIRST PEOPLE: Secrets of Crawford Lake

The summer after grade eight, a friend and I rode our bikes from Lorne Park, near Oakville, to just south of Mount Nemo — quite the outing on only one-speed bikes. It was my first visit to the Niagara Escarpment in Halton; I was just fourteen years old. Little did I realize that I would return as an archaeologist fourteen years later to begin a research program that would last more than twenty-five years. Crawford Lake's unique character and varved sediments created a rare opportunity to accurately date Native villages and learn more about Ontario's Iroquoian people. Yet after twenty-five years of research, Crawford Lake has only begun to yield its secrets of life in the past. Our investigations have discovered only half of the likely two hundred villages, hamlets, cabins and other sites left by the Iroquoians who settled on or near the escarpment in Halton.

Dr. William D. Finlayson, Archaeologist, Museum of Archaeology, London, Ontario

The Halton watershed was once the domain of Native people. Today, only traces of this early occupation and vibrant culture remain in a landscape etched by time and history. From cryptic signs of human activity concealed in the sediment of Halton's Crawford Lake, scientists have pieced together an important fragment of Ontario's past.

Centuries before Europeans settled in the wilderness of Southern Ontario, Native people cultivated corn, beans and squash. These early agriculturists were the Iroquoians. This group of people, who spoke dialects of the same language, included the Wendat, Petun, and Neutral nations. The Iroquoians lived near the Great Lakes in the southern regions of what is now Ontario. In the early days of European contact, it is estimated that 75,000 Iroquoians inhabited this area. By 1650 most of Ontario's Iroquoians had been scattered from the region or were assimilated into other Native groups.

Centuries later an important scientific discovery at Crawford Lake enriched our knowledge of Iroquoian culture. Embedded in the sediment of Crawford Lake were fossilized corn pollen grains, their origin a mystery. In 1971, Dr. Jock McAndrews, a botanist from the Royal Ontario Museum

Dr. Jock McAndrews and assistant study sediment samples from Crawford Lake.

Conservation Halton

found the pollen grains while studying sediment samples from the lake. A long, hollow tube filled with dry ice was pushed into the lake bottom to capture undisturbed sediment that froze to the outside of the sampling device, known as the "frigid finger."

Crawford Lake's unusual geological evolution makes it a natural time capsule. Known as a meromictic lake, it shares similar physical characteristics with less than one percent of Ontario's lakes. With its great depth of 24 metres and small surface area of 2.5 hectares, Crawford Lake has constantly cold bottom water that is oxygen poor. Protected from wind by the surrounding limestone cliffs and forest, there is limited wave action to circulate the water in the spring and fall. There is very little breakdown by worms, bacteria, crustaceans and insect larvae. Nothing can survive in the oxygen-poor bottom water. Everything that settles to the bottom — leaves, pollen grains, microorganisms — is perfectly preserved in the sediment.

The sediment is deposited in alternating light and dark bands. In spring and early summer months, calcium and lime form a light layer. In autumn, the lake receives a deluge of organic matter that creates a dark layer. Together the layers form a couplet known as a varve. Each varve equals one year, similar to counting the growth rings of a tree. The layers of varves represent a stratified historical record of vegetative changes and human activity in the area surrounding the lake over the past thousand years.

By analyzing the varves, scientists have been able to accurately date the preserved material. Evidence of two episodes of human disturbances were found — a European settlement being the most recent and an earlier occupation that dated between 1350 and 1650. During the earlier period, corn pollen was deposited in three different time spans, with the heaviest concentration found between 1434 and 1459.

With this information, and due to the fact that corn pollen is quite heavy and does not travel far in the wind, scientists were led to believe that there were once cultivated cornfields near Crawford Lake. The combination of scientific data from the lake and Native artifacts collected from nearby farmers' fields soon led archaeologists to the site of the most accurately dated Iroquoian settlement in Canada.

Dr. William Finlayson, now Director of the Museum of Archaeology, in London, Ontario, discovered the site in 1973 and began research that would last more than twenty-five years. During several digs, archaeologists unearthed pieces of pottery with distinctive shapes and decoration, arrowheads, and tools made of stone and bone. Over 10,000 pieces were collected at the site, contributing to our knowledge of Iroquoian culture.

Iroquoian people lived in settlements close to their fields. Some settlements were occupied by over 3,000 people. Crawford Lake, with a population of approximately 250 people, was a small village, possibly a satellite of a larger community. Iroquoians stayed in a village for ten to twenty years. They moved to a new location as the availability of firewood declined, the productivity of the soil was exhausted and hunting opportunities were reduced.

Interior view of Turtle Clan Longhouse, Crawford Lake Conservation Area, Milton. ROB STIMPSON

Longhouses, Iroquoian homes, were constructed with bark, usually cedar, tied to a wooden frame and held down by saplings. They were as high as they were wide, and quite long, with curved roofs. At the Crawford Lake site, the remains of ten longhouses, ranging from 25 to 54 metres long, were found. Members of the same clan lived in each longhouse. Clans were named for animals important to those people, such as the bear, wolf, turtle or hawk. Clan membership was matrilineal — family members traced a common ancestor through the female line. A clan consisted of a woman and her daughters, or a group of sisters, with their husbands and children. Clan matrons, the oldest and most respected women in the clan, distributed food, organized marriages and selected chiefs.

In this agrarian society, men and women shared political and economic responsibilities. Men cleared the fields, hunted, fished, constructed tools and dwellings, traded with other villages, and defended the community. Women planted and harvested the crops, processed leather for clothing, made clay pots and raised the children. They lived harmoniously with nature, respecting the bounty of the land and celebrating the changing seasons.

Today, the Crawford Lake heritage site has the most detailed reconstructed Native village in Ontario. The site provides an opportunity to experience living history by exploring two completely reconstructed and furnished longhouses, and three others in various stages of completion. Gardens, animal hides and pottery vessels create an authentic atmosphere that enables visitors to experience the life and times of Ontario's First Peoples.

An Iroquoian longhouse site is revealed during an archaeological excavation in 1973.

Inset: More than 10,000 artifacts were collected from the Crawford Lake site. Conservation Halton

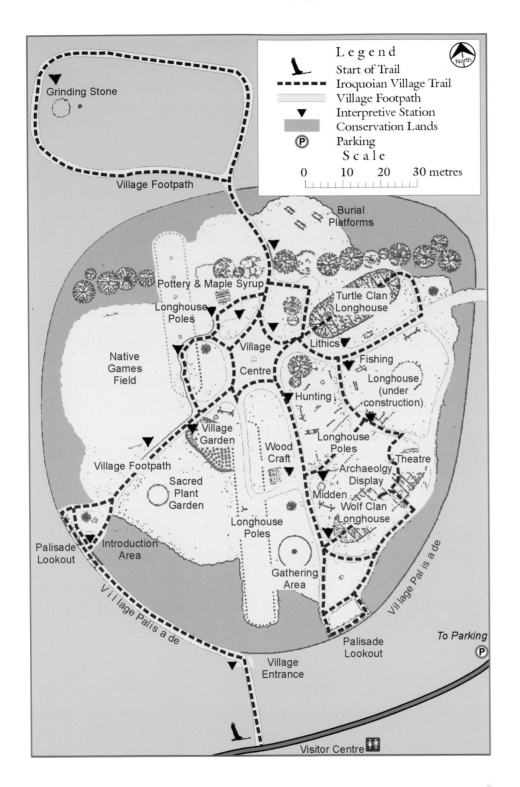

Legend

Start of Trail
Iroquoian Village Trail
Village Footpath
Interpretive Station
Conservation Lands
Ⓟ Parking

Scale

0   10   20   30 metres

Grinding Stone

Village Footpath

Burial Platforms

Pottery & Maple Syrup

Turtle Clan Longhouse

Longhouse Poles

Village Centre

Lithics

Native Games Field

Fishing

Hunting

Longhouse (under construction)

Village Garden

Wood Craft

Longhouse Poles

Theatre

Village Footpath

Archaeolgy Display

Sacred Plant Garden

Midden

Wolf Clan Longhouse

Longhouse Poles

Palisade Lookout

Introduction Area

Gathering Area

Village Palisade

Village Palisade

Palisade Lookout

To Parking
Ⓟ

Village Entrance

Visitor Centre

Watershed Guidepost
Iroquoian Village, Crawford Lake, Milton

The Crawford Lake Conservation Area was once home to Iroquoian people. Today, visitors can step back in time, imagining village life centuries ago as they walk through a reconstructed fifteenth-century Native village. The spirit of the Iroquoians still sings here.

Interpretive stations along the Iroquoian Village Trail convey aspects of Iroquoian culture and how these early people lived in harmony with nature. Two of the five longhouses — Turtle and Wolf Clan — are completely restored. Inside the Turtle Clan Longhouse, the smell of wood smoke, animal hides and tools recall the daily existence of the Iroquoians. The Wolf Clan Longhouse, which has a simulated dig site and exhibits on Native life, helps visitors understand the science of archaeology and the lives of the village's previous inhabitants.

Seeing the village during each season provides much insight into the lifestyles of Ontario's Native people. Visitors can even don snowshoes in the middle of winter and participate in a guided hike that is part of a year-round education program at the conservation area.

Directions: From Highway 401, take Guelph Line south (Exit 312) to Steeles Avenue, then turn east to the park entrance. From the QEW, take Guelph Line north (Exit 102) to Steeles Avenue, then turn east to the park entrance.

Nature Calls - Belted Kingfisher

A walk around Crawford Lake on the elevated boardwalk can be therapeutic and a complete study of nature at the same time. Careful observation at the edge of the clear emerald lake will reveal shadowy fish, mostly bass, darting in and out of the dappled shade of the treelined lake. Listen for the loud rattling sound of the belted kingfisher. This is no ordinary hunter of fish. This large, crested blue bird's unusual call often announces its spectacular head-first dive into the lake. As the kingfisher emerges with fish speared on beak, you can almost imagine a time long ago when the Iroquoians listened to the same sound as they too fished for food at the still lake's edge.

ROBERT MCCAW

VISITORS EXPLORE THE RECONSTRUCTED IROQUOIAN VILLAGE AT CRAWFORD LAKE CONSERVATION AREA, MILTON. SANDY BELL

THE STILL WATERS OF CRAWFORD LAKE REFLECT MUCH OF THE HISTORY OF THE NIAGARA ESCARPMENT, MILTON. MALCOM HOPKINSON

Inset: VISITORS ENJOY THE BOARDWALK THAT SURROUNDS CRAWFORD LAKE, MILTON. CONSERVATION HALTON

A SNAPPING TURTLE GLIDES THROUGH AZURE WATERS OF CRAWFORD LAKE, CRAWFORD LAKE CONSERVATION AREA, MILTON. GORD WOOD

Sugar Bush, Mountsberg Conservation Area, Campbellville. Conservation Halton

3

EARLY PIONEERS
Sugaring Off at Mountsberg

When I recall maple-sugaring time, I hear the snorting of horses and feel the crunch of last year's leaves beneath the granular late-spring snow. The warm spring sun shines through a barren tracery of branches, casting filigree shadow patterns on the ground. I know that in a few weeks the woods will come alive with wildflowers, but the only signs of life for now are the running sap and perhaps an early returning migrant such as a yellow-rumped warbler. Inside the sugar house, acrid wood smoke mixes with the sweet smell of maple vapours, reputed to be a sure-fire cure for a spring cold. Such memories evoke for me a simpler time, when communal labour was a regular part of most people's lives.

RICK ARCHBOLD, AUTHOR OF ROBERT BATEMAN'S NATURAL WORLDS

Sugaring-off is a quintessential Canadian experience. Sugar maples are unique to North America. The Halton watershed has an abundance of maple woodlots where early farmers tapped trees to draw the sweet sap for maple syrup. These sugar bushes are still visible along country roads — the settlers' legacy woven into the landscape. Today's sap harvest provides a glimpse into the pioneer culture of Halton's frontier days.

In the 1700s, the Mississauga nation controlled most of Southern Ontario. The Mississauga were originally Ojibway, part of the Algonkian linguistic group who inhabited the northern Precambrian Shield. After the American Revolution, an influx of United Empire Loyalists into Upper Canada placed pressure on the British government for more land resources for settlement. At the request of the British, the Mississauga surrendered portions of their land in exchange for a steady supply of European trade goods, on which the Mississauga had become dependent.

By 1805 Loyalist settlements had spread to the Burlington Bay area. As more settlers arrived in Upper Canada, the British purchased land along the northern shoreline of Lake Ontario, known as the Mississauga Tract, to satisfy demands. In 1818 the Mississauga nation, decimated by disease, sold the interior section of this tract of land.

Before this extensive European settlement, a primeval forest of oak, pine and maples thrived. Wildlife abounded. Europeans, however, brought with them a land-use ethic different from that of the Native people, and a new language to describe their relationship with the land. In an effort to tame the land, trees were harvested for lumber and forests cleared for fields, swamps were drained, and streams

Sap is collected in wooden buckets and transferred to a barrel on a horse-drawn sled, Mountsberg Conservation Area, Campbellville.
CONSERVATION HALTON

diverted for mills. For the settlers, survival often meant triumph over nature. The sugar bush was as much a part of their survival as wheat fields and waterpower.

In the backwoods of Upper Canada, settlers encountered enormous hardship, including an unforgiving terrain, disease and isolation. It was an arduous life that demanded self-reliance and resourcefulness. Farm tools and cooking utensils were primitive; clothing and furniture were homemade. It was an endless cycle of hard work and near starvation.

The first harvest, beginning the seasonal cycle, was maple sap. Native North Americans introduced Europeans to the art of making maple sugar. Initially, settlers adopted the Native methods, which involved boiling the sap with hot rocks placed in hollowed-out logs. Later the settlers employed their own innovations, such as multiple kettles and the flat pan. With each new innovation, sap processing became more efficient. The invention of a flue-type evaporator in the 1880s made boiling the sap easier. A modified version of this early evaporator is still used on many farms today.

The sap harvest was an enterprise of small-scale economics. Only two species of maples contain sap sweet enough to make maple syrup: the sugar maple and the black maple, which is less common. Sugar maples take thirty to sixty years to reach tappable size. A 35-metre mature tree with a trunk diameter of 120 centimetres can sustain four taps and yield 180 litres of sap per year. It takes 30 to 40 litres of sap to make 1 litre of maple syrup.

The pioneers produced maple sugar primarily because cane sugar was expensive and difficult to procure in rural Ontario. Every pioneer woman was familiar with the importance of maple sugar. It was used in everything from pies, puddings, preserves, cornmeal mush, and cured meats to tea and coffee. The 1861 census reported that Canadian farmers produced six million kilograms of maple sugar, almost completely for family consumption. Maple products were also essential as a supplement to the pioneers' diet. Maple syrup contains vitamin C and may have helped to prevent scurvy over the long winter months.

Signalling the end of winter's isolation, the three to six weeks of the sugaring-off season were a festive time. For Native people and settlers alike, it was an important date on the seasonal calendar. Native people held special ceremonies during the sweet-water season, and settlers invited neighbouring families to help with the harvest. It was a time for celebration as the pioneers eagerly awaited the promise of spring and nature's rebirth.

The maple sap harvest remains a time for celebration. Every year thousands of people visit the Mountsberg Conservation Area to enjoy an authentic Canadian sugaring-off. For the older generation, the sap harvest evokes memories of a simpler time and for children, it is steeped in the magic of spring. Sugaring-off endures as a symbol of Ontario's rural past.

Pioneers used iron kettles to boil sap,
Mountsberg Conservation Area, Campbellville.
CONSERVATION HALTON

THE AFTERGLOW OF A WINTER ICE STORM AT A HALTON FARM, BURLINGTON. SANDY BELL

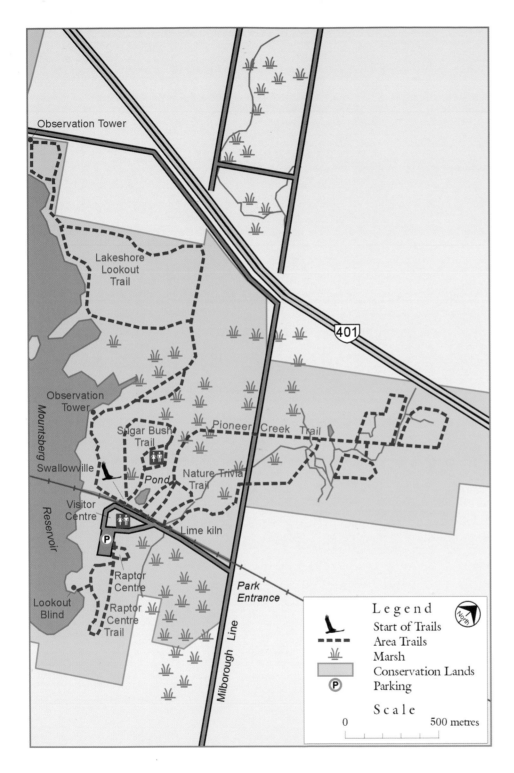

Watershed Guidepost
Mountsberg Conservation Area, Campbellville

With its 14 kilometres of trails for hiking and cross-country skiing, the Mountsberg Conservation Area is a great place to explore and experience nature. Along the Lakeshore Lookout Trail, visitors can observe some of the hundreds of bird species recorded at the conservation area. The Pioneer Creek and Nature Trivia Trails also include unique features that convey the natural history of the park. Mountsberg trails are outfitted with boardwalks, birdfeeders and interpretive lookouts.

During March and April, visitors can enjoy the first taste of spring at the Mountsberg Sugar Bush. The trail to the sugar bush passes by a 120-year-old house and barn built by the Camerons. Archibald Cameron's family first settled in East Flamborough in 1833. His son Duncan Cameron purchased 40 hectares and constructed the stone house and barn that is now part of the conservation area. Interpretive plaques and displays along the Sugarbush Trail tell the story of the maple syrup harvest. Visitors can relive the early settlers' first rite of spring by walking through the hardwood forest and touring the sugar house, where the smell of smoke and steaming sap conjure up nostalgic images of past times.

Directions: From Highway 401, take Guelph Line south (Exit 312) to Reid Side Road, west to Second Side Road, south to Campbellville Road, west to Milborough Line, then turn north to park entrance. From the QEW, take Guelph Line north (Exit 102) to Campbellville Road, west to Milborough Line, then turn north to the park entrance.

Nature Calls - Yellow-Bellied Sapsucker

When you walk quietly through the sugar bush during a good sap run, you can actually hear the sap dripping into the traditional metal buckets. You may also hear the tapping sound of one of nature's critters that is very interested in the maple harvest. Look closely in the direction of the sound and you may see the yellow-bellied sapsucker. This small woodpecker drills orderly rows of holes into a tree and then laps up the sap with its brush-like tongue. The woodpecker's red cap and yellow breast are a welcome dash of colour in the dull, grey woods. The sapsucker arrives in early April and seems to know just when the sap is oozing out of the trees during those first warm, sunny days of spring.

ROBERT McCAW

Visitors enjoy the first taste of spring in the sugar bush at the Mountsberg Conservation Area, Campbellville. Neil Hester

SPRUCE LANE HISTORICAL FARMHOUSE, BRONTE CREEK PROVINCIAL PARK, OAKVILLE. SANDY BELL

Rocking chairs on the veranda conjure up images of times past, Spruce Lane Farm, Bronte Creek Provincial Park, Oakville. Maggie Mills

Rattlesnake Point Conservation Area, Milton. Neil Hester

4

HALTON'S BACKBONE: The Niagara Escarpment

When I was growing up in Oakville, my parents would take me on hikes along the newly formed Bruce Trail to take in some spectacular views. And what a view one gets from the cliffs at Hilton Falls, Mount Nemo, Rattlesnake Point and Kelso. My father and I would talk about the grinding mass of ice that melted earlier in the week — geologically speaking of course! What I didn't know at the time was that one of the most interesting parts of the entire landscape was right at my feet, at the edge of all those cliffs. In fact, it would take half a career as a professional ecologist for me to realize that one of the most significant ecological challenges and opportunities for me was within inches of my fingers when I was only ten years old. After years of studying cliff ecosystems, my students and I realized that we had discovered the most ancient and least-disturbed forest in eastern North America. Nothing will ever match the euphoria of 1988 when the truth about this cedar forest was beginning to be revealed to us. To be able to see my boyhood hometown from the research site also added a sense of poignancy that I wish everyone could experience.

DR. DOUG LARSON, ECOLOGY PROFESSOR, UNIVERSITY OF GUELPH

The Niagara Escarpment towers high above Halton's fertile countryside and urban communities. It gives shape and contour to the landscape. Stretching 725 kilometres from Queenston to Tobermory, the escarpment is an oasis of "wilderness" in the most densely populated region of Canada. The escarpment is the dominant landmark in the Halton watershed, a dramatic expanse of rocks, forests and valleys.

The escarpment has evolved over 450 million years. It originated in the Paleozoic era when rivers laden with mud, sand and clay flowed from ancient mountains — the ancestors of the Appalachians — to an inland sea and deposited their detritus in deltas. These deltas, concentrated in what today is New York state and Ontario, became the foundations of the escarpment.

Millions of years later, a shallow tropical sea covered most of North America. Coral reefs similar to Australia's Great Barrier Reef developed. Plants and primitive sea creatures flourished. As these organisms died, their calcium-

An ancient white cedar tree clings to the edge of the Niagara Escarpment, Rattlesnake Point Conservation Area, Milton.
NEIL HESTER

rich skeletons settled to the ocean floor. Over time the sediment was compressed into the layers of escarpment rock: shale, sandstone, limestone and dolomite.

The ancient sea receded 250 million years ago, leaving the rock exposed to the forces of erosion. Rivers carved narrow valleys into the face of the escarpment. The softer shales weathered more quickly than the resilient dolomite, creating characteristic escarpment landforms: imposing cliffs, magnificent waterfalls, and the enigmatic "flowerpots" of the Bruce Peninsula.

Later in the Pleistocene epoch or "Ice Age," the glaciers further sculpted the escarpment. During this time, the land was buried beneath 2 to 3 kilometres of ice. As the glaciers alternately advanced and retreated, they deepened river valleys and deposited fragments of rocks, sand and clay. The glaciers' final retreat from Southern Ontario and the Niagara Escarpment occurred 12,000 years ago.

These geological transformations molded the escarpment landscape with distinctive features such as Mount Nemo,

Rattlesnake Point, Crawford Lake, Hilton Falls, the Kelso bluffs — birthmarks of exquisite beauty. As the escarpment meanders through Southern Ontario, its complexion changes from rolling hills to imposing rock face; extensive woodlands to pristine wetlands; spectacular waterfalls to productive farmland. Within this mosaic of landscapes, there are a variety of habitats. Natural areas of the escarpment in the Halton watershed alone contain a rich diversity of flora and fauna: more than 150 species of birds; 30 species of reptiles and amphibians; 35 species of mammals; over 60 species of fish; and over 800 species of flora, including 20 types of wild orchids. It is a ribbon of wild land within Canada's industrial heartland.

Species of flora and fauna unique to the region are found in Halton's escarpment habitats. The mature forests of Hilton Falls provide habitat for the provincially rare West Virginia white butterfly. In the caves of Mount Nemo and Rattlesnake Point, two provincially uncommon bats, the small-footed bat and the eastern pipistrelle, have been found. The cool, shaded crevices of Mount Nemo support the nationally and provincially rare hart's tongue fern. As well, the rugged cliffs of Crawford Lake and Rattlesnake Point are an important migratory route for turkey vultures and other birds of prey. Halton's conservation lands also sustain habitats for other rare species, such as the green violet, ginseng, and the slender cliff-brake fern.

The casual visitor is fortunate to witness these natural wonders. Yet for years many people may have unwittingly overlooked the most extensive old-growth forest east of the Rockies. Growing out of the inhospitable cliff face in the Milton area are ancient eastern white cedars. In 1988 Dr. Doug Larson, a University of Guelph professor, discovered cedars up to seven hundred years old. These stunted, twisted trees — some no more than a

Dr. Doug Larson uses a core sampler to age an eastern white cedar tree on the Niagara Escarpment, Milton.
UNIVERSITY OF GUELPH

metre tall and a few centimetres in diameter — are two to three times older than the average for the species. They are among the slowest-growing plants in the world. Further investigation revealed that this ancient forest spanned the entire length of the escarpment and that the trees reached ages exceeding 1,800 years.

The tenacity of these cedars is remarkable. The marginal habitat of rocks and shallow soil in which the cedars eke out an existence is partially responsible for their survival. The isolation of the cliff face has protected them from fire and other natural disturbances, and its inaccessibility has prevented human interference. While other old-growth forests were stripped for lumber or cleared for fields, these diminutive cedars were ignored. The cedars are hundreds of years older than other trees in Ontario, making them a valuable storehouse of information. Tree-ring records can provide scientists with important data about climate patterns. With this information, scientists may be able to decipher trends in climate change, global warming and air-pollution levels.

The international significance of the Niagara Escarpment was recognized in 1990 when the United Nations Educational, Scientific, and Cultural Organization declared the Niagara Escarpment a World Biosphere Reserve. The escarpment joins other famous World Biosphere Reserves such as the Serengeti Plain, the Galapagos Islands and the Florida Everglades.

For thousands of years, the sentinel cliffs of Mount Nemo and Rattlesnake Point have held a silent vigil over the Halton watershed, witnessing and recording changes to the land. The Niagara Escarpment continues to require the constant vigilance of a concerned public to protect its treasured habitat.

THE NIAGARA ESCARPMENT MEANDERS THROUGH THE HALTON COUNTRYSIDE. THIS VIEW OF MOUNT NEMO IS FROM RATTLESNAKE POINT. NEIL HESTER

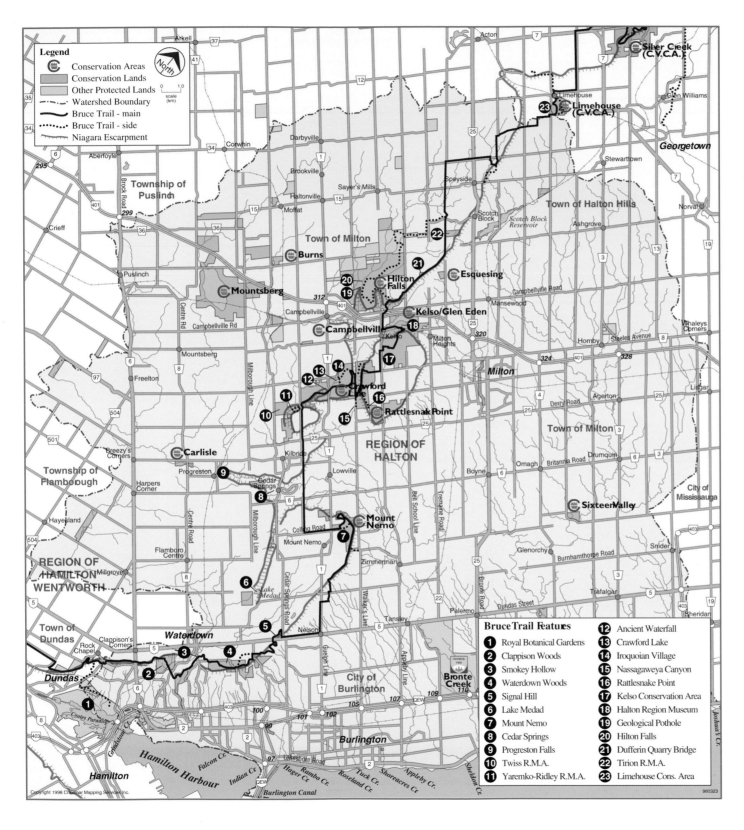

Bruce Trail Features

#	Feature	#	Feature
1	Royal Botanical Gardens	12	Ancient Waterfall
2	Clappison Woods	13	Crawford Lake
3	Smokey Hollow	14	Iroquoian Village
4	Waterdown Woods	15	Nassagaweya Canyon
5	Signal Hill	16	Rattlesnake Point
6	Lake Medad	17	Kelso Conservation Area
7	Mount Nemo	18	Halton Region Museum
8	Cedar Springs	19	Geological Pothole
9	Progreston Falls	20	Hilton Falls
10	Twiss R.M.A.	21	Dufferin Quarry Bridge
11	Yaremko-Ridley R.M.A.	22	Tirion R.M.A.
		23	Limehouse Cons. Area

Watershed Guidepost
The Bruce Trail

The Bruce Trail, stretching 725 kilometres from Niagara to Tobermory, provides unique opportunities to appreciate the beauty of the Niagara Escarpment. It is the oldest and longest marked hiking trail in Canada.

In the Halton watershed, the Bruce Trail starts at the Royal Botanical Gardens near Dundas and extends to Halton Hills just east of Acton. This 75-kilometre stretch of the Bruce Trail winds through charming communities and features sparkling waterfalls, pristine lakes and massive limestone cliffs.

The Bruce Trail provides endless hiking opportunities through breathtaking landscapes and is accessible from most of the conservation lands of the Halton watershed. Becoming a member of the Bruce Trail Association and purchasing a trail guide with detailed maps is a great investment. Go for an hour's walk, a full-day hike or begin a family project of hiking the entire Halton section of the trail over a season or two.

Directions: The Bruce Trail can be reached from many locations throughout the Halton watershed, including Rattlesnake Point, Hilton Falls, Kelso and Mount Nemo Conservation Areas. The main trail is marked with white blazes painted on trees, and numerous side trails to interesting features are marked with blue blazes. The Bruce Trail often shares the same trails established at conservation areas as well as on local roads and on some private lands by special agreement with landowners.

ROBERT McCAW

Nature Calls - Red Squirrels and Ancient Cedars

As you hike the Bruce Trail and experience some of those inspiring cliff-edge views, don't miss one of Halton's most interesting natural features right underfoot. The white cedars that line the edge of the Niagara Escarpment are part of Ontario's oldest-growth forest. Some of these trees are more than a thousand years old, their growth stunted because of the harsh climate at the escarpment's edge. This incredible old-growth forest can be seen along the entire escarpment as a ruffled ribbon of rich green. Among the cedars, you will often hear and see one of nature's most active and noisy creatures, the red squirrel. This squirrel chatters with curiosity, chips with surprise and scolds with a loud guttural trill that lets you know when you're on its turf.

HIKING ON THE BRUCE TRAIL,
NEAR GRINDSTONE CREEK, TOWN OF FLAMBOROUGH.
NEIL HESTER

HIKERS MAKE THEIR WAY THROUGH RICH GREENERY AT THE BASE OF A LIMESTONE CLIFF AT MOUNT NEMO CONSERVATION AREA, BURLINGTON. UNIVERSITY OF GUELPH

Rose-breasted Grosbeak. Robert McCaw

MOLLY THE DOG EXPLORES PICTURESQUE BRONTE CREEK. PAT AND ROSEMARIE KEOUGH

5

HIDDEN TREASURES OF BRONTE CREEK

When I began research for my book on Bronte Creek, I discovered that there are indeed treasures along its route, far more treasures than I had ever imagined! I thought the creek had only one source, in Beverly Swamp, but I discovered that it has many, each with its own special delights. Take, for example, the remnants of the vanished village of Progreston near Carlisle. This little community was named over 125 years ago to let the world know that the busy mills along the creek reflected the most modern technology of the time. Nearby was another tiny industrial settlement hidden away in a forest glen where the creek is a splendid sight. No wonder the Neutral Indians chose to settle here, on the banks of a creek, where they had everything at hand — fish, game, fine soil, good water and absolutely beautiful surroundings.

DOROTHY TURCOTTE, AUTHOR OF *PLACES AND PEOPLE ON BRONTE CREEK*

Bronte Creek flows through the history of the Halton watershed, reflecting clues of its colourful natural and cultural heritage. It rises from the rich wetlands of the northwest part of the watershed and gains force as the creek's twelve tributaries merge. On its meandering path, Bronte Creek passes vanished villages and quaint hamlets. Each village is a testament to the stalwart pioneers who, captivated by the potential of the creek, settled this area. Today Bronte Creek has retired from its hardworking pioneer days. It now teems with wildlife and charms city dwellers and outdoor enthusiasts alike.

A tour through the Bronte Creek watershed naturally begins at the headwaters. The tributaries of Bronte Creek originate in the "swamps" of Badenoch and Beverly. Wetlands are now recognized as a crucial part of the watershed ecosystem and as a significant habitat for wildlife. Nineteenth-century settlers, however, did not see the intrinsic ecological value of wetlands. Wetlands were considered an impediment to settlement, with Beverly Swamp even known as the "terror of travellers." These wetlands are now a naturalist's paradise, brimming with birds, amphibians and rare plants.

A green heron looks for fish at the water's edge. ROBERT McCAW

Another tributary begins near the forgotten village of Darbyville in Nassagaweya Township. This tributary crosses into Puslinch Township close to Moffat. An interesting anecdote is that Moffat was once nicknamed "Gomorrah," and Haltonville, where a tiny settlement still exists, was called "Sodom." It is possible the villages received these nicknames because of the settlers' hard-drinking habits. In the 1870s, the Sons of Temperance tried to close down many local taverns — Sodom and Gomorrah were among their targets.

A little-known treasure of Bronte Creek can be found on the west side of the Mountsberg Conservation Area where a tributary has been dammed to create a 202-hectare reservoir for water control and wildlife. Standing alone, hidden among a thick grove of cedar trees is a tall, rose-coloured brick chimney that was once part of a thriving sawmill powered by Bronte Creek. The sawmill was built by Thomas McCrae and Company in 1850 and later passed to his son David. After his career in the army, David's son, Lieutenant Colonel John McCrae, became famous for writing "In Flander's Fields," the best-known poem of World War I.

As this web of tributaries — flowing from Nassageweya Township, Morriston, Beverly and Mountsberg — unites with the main creek, it swells into a picturesque river. A scenic stop on its meandering journey is the village of Carlisle. In the 1960s, the Twelve Mile Creek Conservation Authority, which later became the Halton Region Conservation Authority, acquired four hectares to protect the flood plain. Today, the Carlisle Conservation Area is a great spot to picnic or fish, or just enjoy Bronte Creek as it twists past hamlets and ghost towns on its way towards Lake Ontario.

The banks of Bronte Creek were once speckled with small villages that depended on waterpower for their survival. Nascent communities such as Progreston, upstream from Lowville, flourished because of their location along the creek. A 1.5-metre waterfall at Progreston made it a natural choice for a mill complex. Over the years Progreston had grist-, saw-, woollen, feed and shingle mills. As the creek passes the ruins of an old mill, it flows under a canopy of wilderness forest toward the vanished villages of Cumminsville and Dakota.

The historical Dakota Mill was destroyed by fire many years ago. Cedar Springs, Burlington. ROBERT BATEMAN

The Hamilton Powder Company, which produced explosives, was located in Dakota. The company employed over 200 men from Cumminsville, Dakota and Kilbride. A peg factory in Progreston produced maple pegs for the workers' shoes because workers could not wear shoes with metal nails in the explosives plant due to the danger of sparks. Tragically, in 1884 an explosion in the plant killed five men and devastated the community. People in Owen Sound, Hamilton and St. Catharines claim to have felt the explosion. The plant was never rebuilt and the operation was moved to Montreal. Slowly, families moved away from Cumminsville and Dakota to find other employment. In 1927 William Delos Flatt purchased the powder company property to build cottages for a summer retreat. Today many of the cottages remain in the Cedar Springs community, a hidden natural enclave amid the rapidly growing City of Burlington.

After leaving the Cedar Springs valley, Bronte Creek continues eastward past rich farmland to Zimmerman and on to Bronte Creek Provincial Park. On its 50-kilometre journey from the headwaters, Bronte Creek follows the path that the glaciers carved thousands of years ago. Spectacular evidence of the glaciers is the gorge in the provincial park. During the Ice Age, meltwaters from the retreating glaciers flowed toward glacial Lake Iroquois and carved the gorge. Running in the same direction as Bronte Creek is an ancient buried ravine that the advancing glaciers filled with debris. William Lyon Mackenzie, the leader of the Rebellion of 1837, is purported to have hidden in a cave here while fleeing to the United States. Other Ontario caves also claim this historical honour.

At the mouth of Bronte Creek is the village of Bronte. In 1820 the Mississauga chiefs surrendered their hunting and fishing rights on the reserves at the mouth of Bronte and Sixteen Mile Creeks. This surrender opened the land to European settlement. Rather than through a private sale, the land was sold at a public auction in 1826. Joseph Hixon purchased the land for a mill site but did not build one here. It was not until Samuel Bealey Harrison, who arrived in 1837, obtained Hixon's mill site that Bronte had grist- and sawmills. Harrison continued to promote Bronte's economic development. He petitioned the House of Assembly to construct

SALEM PIONEER CEMETERY NEAR BRONTE CREEK, BURLINGTON. SANDY BELL

At right: BRONTE CREEK VALLEY,
BRONTE CREEK PROVINCIAL PARK, OAKVILLE. NEIL HESTER

a harbour at Bronte. After his petition was granted, the Bronte Harbour Company was formed, and the harbour was finished in 1856.

During the nineteenth century, Bronte Harbour boomed with shipments of grain and wheat. The wheat boom ended with the arrival of the Grand Trunk Railway. Farmers now took their grain to rail yards instead of the lakeshore. Unlike many communities, Bronte survived the ascendency of trains. It developed boatbuilding, fishing and stone-hooking industries. Today, as part of the Town of Oakville, Bronte has a vibrant waterfront life.

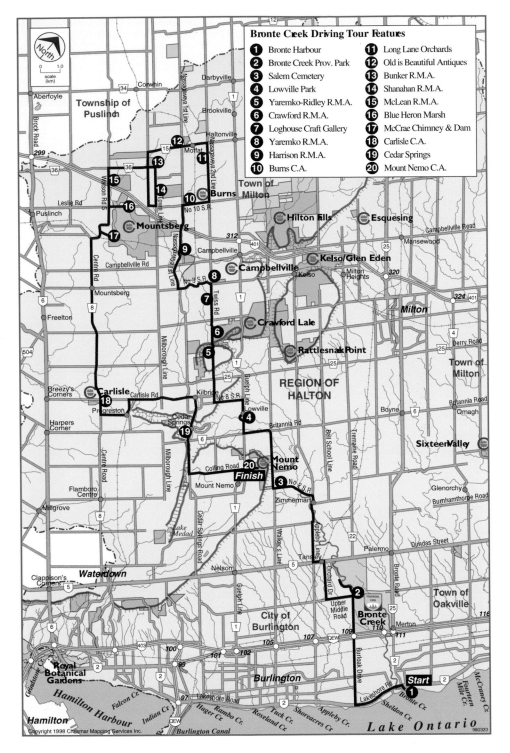

Bronte Creek Driving Tour Features

1. Bronte Harbour
2. Bronte Creek Prov. Park
3. Salem Cemetery
4. Lowville Park
5. Yaremko-Ridley R.M.A.
6. Crawford R.M.A.
7. Loghouse Craft Gallery
8. Yaremko R.M.A.
9. Harrison R.M.A.
10. Burns C.A.
11. Long Lane Orchards
12. Old is Beautiful Antiques
13. Bunker R.M.A.
14. Shanahan R.M.A.
15. McLean R.M.A.
16. Blue Heron Marsh
17. McCrae Chimney & Dam
18. Carlisle C.A.
19. Cedar Springs
20. Mount Nemo C.A.

Watershed Guidepost
Bronte Creek Driving Tour

The Bronte Creek watershed is endowed with many splendid natural and historical treasures. This scenic driving tour through the watershed begins at Bronte Harbour and proceeds northwest past Bronte Creek Provincial Park, through the forgotten communities of Tansley and Zimmerman, and then by the Salem pioneer cemetery. From here you have a spectacular view of Mount Nemo on your way to historic Lowville, where you can walk along the creek in Lowville Park. The tour continues on back roads by conservation lands known as Yaremko-Ridley and Crawford Resource Management Areas. Along the way, you pass the Loghouse Craft Gallery and other conservation lands including, Yaremko-Ridley and Harrison Resource Management Areas and the Burns Conservation Area, where you can hike along a boardwalk through a beautiful wetland. At the northern reach of the drive, near Moffat, you pass Long Lane Orchards' pick-your-own farm and the Old is Beautiful Antiques shop. Now in the headwaters of Bronte Creek, the return journey passes by the Bunker, Shanahan and McLean Resource Management Areas to the Blue Heron Marsh and McCrae Chimney, located on the north and west sides of the Mountsberg Conservation Area. Further south, at the Carlisle Conservation Area, you travel east through the charming communities of Progreston, Kilbride and Cedar Springs before the tour ends at the Mount Nemo Conservation Area. This 90-kilometre scenic drive takes about two hours. Be prepared to tour much longer if you explore the twenty highlighted sites along the way. You may want to travel the route in sections over several days or in different seasons, particularly during the fall colour change. The route shown on the map crosses or runs along the creek in many locations. Watch for jogs or loops off the main route as you discover Bronte Creek's many hidden treasures.

Directions: From the QEW, take Bronte Road south (Exit 111) to the village of Bronte and Bronte Harbour.

Nature Calls - Bufflehead and Sandpipers

Blue Heron Marsh, at the north end of the Mountsberg Reservoir, is a great place to see marsh and shore birds. There is a lookout tower and causeway where birders use binoculars and telescopes to spot numerous species of waterbirds. During spring, look for blue- and green-winged teal, hooded mergansers and bufflehead ducks, and listen for the *oh ger glee* whistles of red-winged blackbirds, which are ubiquitous.

During the fall, the extensive mud flats of the reservoir attract shorebirds such as sandpipers, plovers and phalaropes. These wading birds are constantly moving and tipping in search of food. They're fun to watch and to listen to. They make a variety of peeping sounds as they often fly together in jet-like formation, dashing from mud flat to mud flat.

ROBERT MCCAW

A HIKER ENJOYS MARSH MARIGOLDS IN FULL BLOOM FROM THE WETLAND BOARDWALK, BURNS CONSERVATION AREA, MILTON. ROB STIMPSON

SALMON FISHING IN BRONTE CREEK, OAKVILLE. NEIL HESTER

Canoeing on Bronte Creek near Bronte Harbour, Oakville. Lori Labatt

In search of the elusive salmon in Sixteen Mile Creek, Lions Valley Park, Oakville. Rob Boak

6

THE SIXTEEN MILE CREEK MYSTERY TOUR

During high-water conditions, Sixteen Mile Creek is known throughout Ontario as a premier whitewater river. Hidden away in the Golden Horseshoe, the creek retains much of its wilderness beauty. I was first introduced to its challenging rapids in the early 1970s. Twenty-five years later, during lower water flows, my children and I have encountered all kinds of wildlife, fascinating fish runs, and bird migrations that few people take the time to watch or even know exist. When paddling from Hilton Falls to Lake Ontario, one encounters the many faces of Sixteen Mile Creek, from a fast-moving trout stream in a wilderness setting to a raging, unforgiving whitewater river. The best part is that it flows right through the heart of Halton, to be enjoyed, respected and, I hope, preserved for future generations.

JEFF McCOLL, CANOE ENTHUSIAST AND NATIONAL KAYAK CHAMPION

Sixteen Mile Creek has many faces — sometimes a lovely wilderness stream and at other times a raging whitewater river. The creek's three branches — West, Middle and East — flow through various habitats, from wetlands, rich forests and pastures to deep ravines, before eventually converging en route to Oakville Harbour. The habitats within this watershed are an invaluable ecological resource. Seven Environmentally Sensitive Areas are located within the watershed boundaries, and numerous threatened or vulnerable species, such as the Cooper's hawk, spotted turtle, southern flying squirrel, and eastern bluebird, inhabit the area.

On its journey from the headwaters, Sixteen Mile Creek unites the towns of Milton, Halton Hills and Oakville in a web of wetlands, streams and human communities. Some of the communities along the creek, such as Milton and Oakville, have flourished, while others endure only as road signs or as footnotes in the dusty pages of historical texts. These vanished villages and their cemeteries still convey much information about the early days of human settlement.

Rail line through an autumn forest near Sixteen Mile Creek, Campbellville. SANDY BELL

Our tour along Sixteen Mile Creek begins on its western boundary where a tributary of the West Branch originates near the village of Campbellville on Guelph Line. The Canadian Pacific Railway was built through Campbellville in 1880, and in the decades that followed the community prospered with several stores, hotels and a brick plant that was later converted to a sawmill by Murray Crawford. Campbellville was the business and cultural centre for the southern portion of Nassagaweya Township. Although its days of industrial progress have faded, Campbellville is still a quaint village, attracting tourists and antique hunters. A unique feature of the village — one that can easily be overlooked — is the small pond in the Campbellville Conservation Area. The pond has a natural cleaning system by way of a mini-wetland. Runoff from roads and sidewalks flows through the wetland system and is cleaned by natural vegetation such as cattails, that filter out sediment particles and absorb nutrients and contaminants from the water. The quality of water is improved before it enters the main pond and flows downstream to Kelso. It is a progressive idea that employs nature's expertise to remedy the effects of pollution. As the creek leaves Campbellville, it is surrounded by forest.

The headwaters of another tributary of the West Branch rise from the wetlands within Hilton Falls Conservation Area. This creek cascades over the escarpment, creating a picturesque waterfall known as Hilton Falls. Ruins from an old mill are visible near the base of the waterfall. The creek continues past an unusual geological pothole before entering a large glacial valley. It heads south to converge with the other tributaries at Kelso Lake before flowing through urban Milton.

The headwaters of Middle Branch also arise on the Niagara Escarpment. Atop the escarpment on Highway 25 is the village of Speyside, now a mostly residential area. The only vestige of the old village is the corner store and the road sign. A century ago Speyside was a vibrant town with hotels, a tannery, sawmills, a shingle mill, a school, stores and a stone quarry. From this elevation there is a spectacular view of the countryside, and on a clear day it is possible to see the skyline of Toronto. The Middle Branch of Sixteen Mile Creek continues through Scotch Block Reservoir, named after a nearby community that was once an enclave of Scottish settlers.

The creek's Middle Branch converges with the East Branch upstream from the village of Drumquin. This community was settled about 1820, and soon after, Joseph Howes built the area's first gristmill using waterpower from Sixteen Mile Creek. Sawmills soon followed, as the area abounded in white oak. Today the sand-and-silt soil have made it a prime location for tree nurseries. Golf courses also have found a niche within this otherwise agricultural area. Downstream from Drumquin is the Sixteen Valley

Canoeists create a gentle wake at the mouth of Sixteen Mile Creek, Oakville Harbour. SUSAN HANSON

Conservation Area, located on Lower Base Line in Milton. The Sixteen Mile Creek Valley is one of the richest natural sites in the watershed. Provincially and nationally rare species found there include hawthorn, Virginia yellow flax and burning bush. The conservation area has nature trails for hiking, and chinook salmon and bass provide sport-fishing opportunities. After the two branches converge, the creek deepens and the valley narrows into a beautiful gorge all the way to Lake Ontario.

At the mouth of Sixteen Mile Creek is Oakville Harbour. William Chisholm, Oakville's founding father, was responsible for the commercial harbour and the area's economic growth. Oakville Harbour was the first privately owned harbour in Upper Canada and was once a prosperous and busy port. Between 1855 and 1875, harbour revenue dropped dramatically due to falling wheat prices and the building of the Great Western Railway. By the 1870s, Oakville's days as a great shipping port were over.

Today Oakville is an enchanting town, still linked to the creek and harbour that shaped its past. Recreational sports such as boating have remained popular here since the early 1900s. Olympic medalist and Canadian Hall of Fame inductee Larry Cain, who trained on Sixteen Mile Creek, continues this traditional connection to the river. Cain won the gold medal in the 55-metre singles-canoe event and the silver medal in the 1,000-metre race at the 1984 Olympics. Jeff McColl, six-time national kayak champion, has also explored this creek extensively.

The intimacy with the creek's moods and personalities that is derived from canoeing or kayaking accentuates the connections between nature and humans.

A PROFUSION OF FERNS AND MARSH MARIGOLDS IN THE HEADWATERS OF SIXTEEN MILE CREEK, SPEYSIDE. ROBERT McCAW

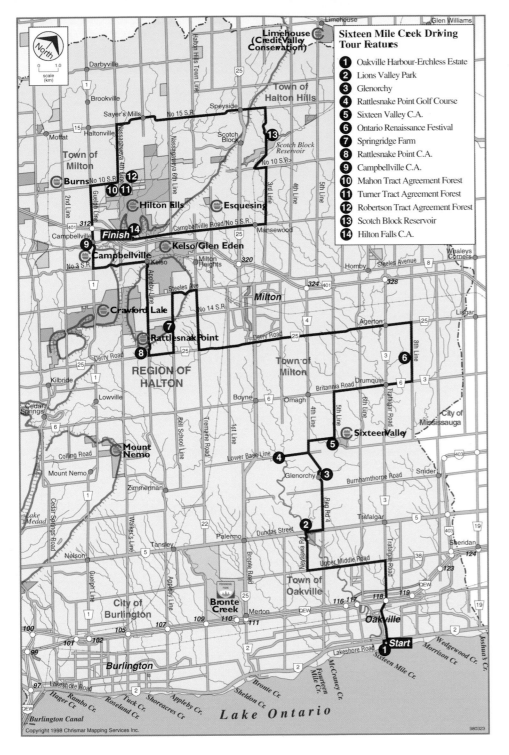

Copyright 1998 Chrismar Mapping Services Inc.

980323

Sixteen Mile Creek Driving Tour Features

1. Oakville Harbour-Erchless Estate
2. Lions Valley Park
3. Glenorchy
4. Rattlesnake Point Golf Course
5. Sixteen Valley C.A.
6. Ontario Renaissance Festival
7. Springridge Farm
8. Rattlesnake Point C.A.
9. Campbellville C.A.
10. Mahon Tract Agreement Forest
11. Turner Tract Agreement Forest
12. Robertson Tract Agreement Forest
13. Scotch Block Reservoir
14. Hilton Falls C.A.

Watershed Guidepost
Sixteen Mile Creek Driving Tour

The Sixteen Mile Creek flows through extensive farmland and developed urban areas where the creek is often difficult to see and appreciate. This driving tour begins at Oakville Harbour, where you can explore a waterfront park and the Erchless Estate, now part of the Oakville Museum. From here the tour winds northwest through Oakville to Lions Valley Park and then on to the hamlet of Glenorchy, where the creek cuts through a beautiful wooded valley. Further north at Lower Base Line, the route jogs west to the Rattlesnake Point Golf Course, where the meandering creek flows through another scenic valley. The tour backtracks east to the Sixteen Valley Conservation Area and then proceeds east through Drumquin, past the Ontario Renaissance Festival site, and then northwest, where the route goes up and down the escarpment by Springridge pick-your-own farm and Rattlesnake Point Conservation Area. Along the way, other conservation lands can be seen as you travel through the hamlet of Kelso and the village of Campbellville. This is a great place to stop and browse the shops or view the west branch of the creek before heading northeast into the creek's headwaters, past several Halton Region agreement forests and through the almost forgotten communities of Sayer's Mills and Speyside. The return journey travels south past the Scotch Block Reservoir, then east to the Hilton Falls Conservation Area where the tour ends.

The 80-kilometre scenic drive takes about two hours and much longer if you explore the sites along the way. The route shown on the map crosses the creek in many locations and sometimes jogs off the main route. The Sixteen Mile Creek driving tour is best done in the summer and fall, as some of the roads are seasonal and may be closed during the winter.

Directions: From the QEW, take Trafalgar Road south (Exit 118) to Lakeshore Road, turn west to Navy Street and travel south to the Erchless Estate and the Oakville Harbour.

Nature Calls - Great Blue Heron Fencing

As you crisscross the picturesque Sixteen Mile Creek on the backroads of the Halton watershed, watch for nature's most impressive fisherman, the stately great blue heron. The long-legged heron will stand on the bank or in the creek without a single movement for long periods of time. Then, ever so slowly, its neck extends to bring its formidable sharp beak into position. With lightning speed, the spearlike beak is thrust below the surface of the water, often reappearing with an impaled fish or frog. The metre-high blue-and-grey bird is an expert fisherman and a thrill to watch. When startled, the heron emits deep, harsh croaks as it laboriously flies away.

ROBERT McCAW

Sixteen Mile Creek flows into Lake Ontario, Oakville Harbour. Geoff Grenville

MAN AND BEST FRIEND GO FISHING ON SIXTEEN MILE CREEK, OAKVILLE. SCOTT ROBERTSON

Sunrise at the light station, Oakville Harbour. Scott Robertson

Sixteen Mile Creek cascades over the Niagara Escarpment, Hilton Falls Conservation Area, Milton. Sandy Bell

7

CHASING WATERFALLS ON HALTON CONSERVATION LANDS

In April 1962, over thirty-five years ago, I was privileged to participate in a trail-blazing hike with six friends who were enthusiastic about a proposed Bruce Trail that would cross Ontario from Queenston to Tobermory, on the tip of the Bruce Peninsula. The old Toronto Telegram *provided transportation and daily front-page coverage of our progress. We started from the Mount Nemo Conservation Area near Burlington. This area and many others in the Halton watershed were all part of this groundbreaking Bruce Trail hike. The 185-kilometre adventure from Halton to Georgian Bay was an astounding contribution to what would become a world-renowned hiking trail. Today the Bruce Trail is a monument to the public agencies who have acquired significant natural lands for conservation, to the private landowners who allow access to the trail, and to the hundreds of volunteers who maintain it. More than ever before, the trail gives us easy access to the natural world and is an antidote to the pressures created by our urban society. Even at eighty-seven years of age, I still get a thrill gazing at a waterfall cascading over the escarpment. It makes me feel young and alive.*

RAY LOWES, FOUNDER OF THE BRUCE TRAIL

hasing waterfalls on Halton conservation lands can be a rewarding pastime. The soothing rhythm of cascading water inspires poetry in even the most prosaic observer. The timeless beauty of waterfalls strikes a chord in all of us, connecting us with the sights and sounds of nature. However, behind the translucent veil of water is a fascinating intersection of geological and human history.

Waterfalls provide significant clues to the geological history of the watershed. Southwest of Crawford Lake, in the centre of Halton Region, is an ancient waterfall that has been dry for at least 12,000 years. As the glaciers retreated, enormous amounts of meltwater were produced and discharged into channels. In the Crawford Lake area, a meltwater channel drained over this fossilized waterfall through a gorge and into a glacial lake. Many streams and rivers still follow these ancient discharge channels.

The forces of erosion have carved waterfalls over millennia. In a process known as sapping, the softer layers of rock, such as shale or sandstone, are eroded, and the layers of harder rock, such as dolostone or

A chestnut-sided warbler shows off its spring plumage. ROBERT MCCAW

limestone, above the softer layers, fall away in large blocks, thereby creating the dramatic vertical faces associated with waterfalls. This process is endless as rivers and streams patiently continue to sculpt the rock.

The Niagara Escarpment has created a number of waterfalls that are worth chasing. As one of the tributaries of Sixteen Mile Creek cascades over the escarpment, it creates the enchanting Hilton Falls. It is a 10-metre-high waterfall with a subtle lure that entices people to witness its seasonal variations, whether it is winter's ice sculptures, summer's lazy trickle or spring's symphony of cascading water. Located in the Hilton Falls Conservation Area, the falls are surrounded by one of the largest natural forest tracts in the Halton watershed.

Hilton Falls is not only a spectacular natural area, it is also a significant cultural heritage site. A legend of gold, said to have been discovered nearby and kept in a cave with iron gates, enhances the falls' natural mystique. Another tale claims that it was a stop on the Underground Railway, an informal network of people who conducted slaves from the United States to freedom in Upper Canada.

Ruins from three mills still exist near the waterfall. The mills are now silent. The ruins, however, are a testimony to the tenacity of the early pioneers in a landscape that was often unwelcoming to human endeavour. Early Ontario settlements and commercial enterprises were often established near waterfalls. Grist-, saw- and woollen mills would harness the power generated by water as it cascaded over the escarpment brow. Until the advent of steam and electricity, waterpower was crucial to the economic development of Upper Canada.

Like many waterfalls, Hilton Falls was named after an early settler and entrepreneur, in this case Edward Hilton. He constructed the first mill at the base of the falls in 1835. The fate of his mill was connected to historical events of the period. Hilton supported William Lyon Mackenzie in the Rebellion of 1837, and after the uprising was quelled, Hilton fled to the United States, leaving his mill to fall into ruin.

In 1856 Dr. George Park acquired the property and built another mill, with an immense 12-metre-diameter waterwheel to power the machinery. The stone ruins indicate a well-built mill. Park sold the operation in 1857, at the same time as the economic boom of the 1850s collapsed. The mill burned in 1860. The final mill, constructed by John Richards, was in operation from 1863 to 1867. There is little record of the mill's history during this period. Today, near these ruins, the forests of Hilton Falls once more grow unimpeded.

Just south of Waterdown, Grindstone Creek flows over the escarpment, creating another scenic treasure at the edge of the Halton watershed. Once a thriving milling complex, the hamlet of Smokey Hollow has vanished with the passage of time. Around 1805 Alexander Brown, who acquired the land originally granted to Alexander McDonnell, built a sawmill above the falls. Other millers soon followed, and the quiet Grindstone Creek valley was transformed into an industrial centre and a smoky hollow. One of Upper Canada's first woollen mills was in Smokey Hollow, but it burned down in 1850 and was never rebuilt.

As was the case with many mills, technological progress — the conversion from waterpower to steam and electricity, and the construction of the railway through the valley in 1912 — signalled the end of Smokey Hollow's industrial boom. All that remains is a plaque beside the waterfall.

Ironically, the success of some water-powered enterprises was also the root of their demise. The forests protected the water supply by slowing the spring runoff and maintaining the summer water table, thus ensuring reliable year-round flows. As the settlers advanced into the wilderness, their deforestation and stream diversion projects altered the water flow. The millstreams were no longer protected — spring snowmelts flooded the river, and in summer the rivers slowed to a trickle. Waterpower was no longer a viable option.

Today nature is slowly reclaiming its lost treasures. The Halton Region Conservation Authority, through its conservation programs, has ensured that the watershed's natural wonders are protected for future generations and that the sound of cascading water will continue to echo through the watershed's forests.

Ruins of three nineteenth-century saw mills create mystery near the falls, Hilton Falls Conservation Area, Milton. ALAN ERNST

G RINDSTONE C REEK TUMBLES OVER THE ESCARPMENT AT S MOKEY H OLLOW, W ATERDOWN. S ANDY B ELL *Inset: A RTIST B RIAN D ARCY'S INSPIRING PAINTING OF S MOKEY H OLLOW, W ATERDOWN.*

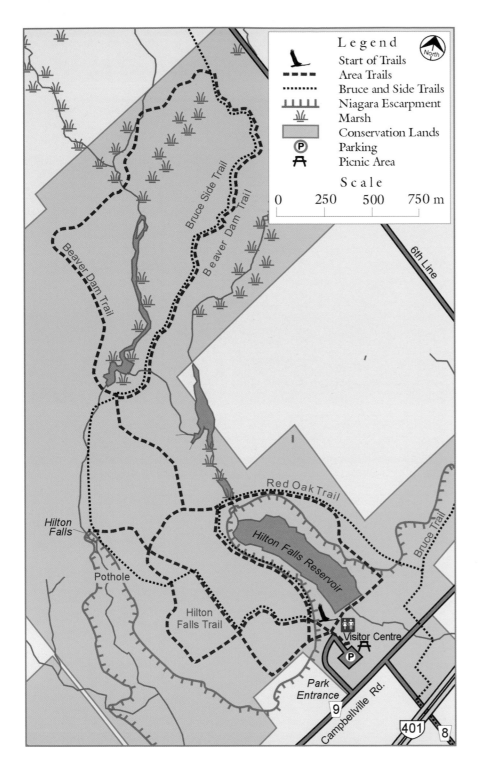

Legend

- Start of Trails
- Area Trails
- Bruce and Side Trails
- Niagara Escarpment
- Marsh
- Conservation Lands
- (P) Parking
- (A) Picnic Area

Scale

0   250   500   750 m

Labels on map: Bruce Side Trail, Beaver Dam Trail, 6th Line, Red Oak Trail, Hilton Falls Reservoir, Bruce Trail, Hilton Falls, Pothole, Hilton Falls Trail, Visitor Centre, Park Entrance, Campbellville Rd., 9, 401, 8

Watershed Guidepost
Hilton Falls Conservation Area, Campbellville

The simple pleasure of watching water cascade over the escarpment at the Hilton Falls Conservation Area is a balm for world-weary spirits. Visitors will also be amazed at the diversity of wildlife they encounter on the trails. A series of three looped trails, varying in length from 2 to 9.5 kilometres, highlight the conservation area's other natural features — wetlands, beaver ponds, forests, and a 12,000-year-old pothole. In the conservation area's diverse habitats, over a hundred species of birds are known to breed, and mammals such as white-tailed deer, beaver and the unusual northern flying squirrel are also found.

The grand beauty of Hilton Falls is juxtaposed with the delicate charm of the conservation area's unique wildflowers, including yellow lady's slipper, showy orchid, walking fern and spleenwort. In spring the woodlands burst forth with a symphony of colour.

With each new season Hilton Falls will astound you with its display of nature's artistry and diversity.

Directions: From Highway 401, take Guelph Line north (Exit 312) to Campbellville Road, then turn east to the park entrance. From the QEW, take Guelph Line north (Exit 102) to Campbellville Road, then turn east to the park entrance.

Nature Calls — Black-Capped Chickadees and Ice Sculptures

People aren't the only ones attracted to the visual and auditory qualities of waterfalls. Wildlife is too, particularly birds such as the black-capped chickadee. While listening to the soothing trickle of water amid the ever-changing ice sculpture at Hilton Falls in winter, take some time to handfeed the chickadees. With energetic, jerky movements and a delightful *chica dee dee dee*, these tame birds will readily come to your hand for a tasty sunflower treat. The experience is a sure cure for the dullest of days and the saddest of hearts. Come back in spring to see the forest's wood warblers — golden-winged, blackburnian and cerulean.

ROBERT McCAW

CHILDREN MARVEL AT THE ICE SCULPTURE CREATED BY A FROZEN WATERFALL AT HILTON FALLS CONSERVATION AREA, MILTON. PHILIP SCHMIDT

BEAVER DAM AND RICH WETLAND, HILTON FALLS CONSERVATION AREA, MILTON. RICHARD ARMSTRONG

A Canada Goose sits on its nest atop a muskrat house, Hilton Falls Conservation Area, Milton. Robert McCaw

MILTON HEIGHTS, KELSO CONSERVATION AREA, MILTON. NEIL HESTER

LEGENDARY PROMONTORIES: Kelso and Rattlesnake Point

Rattlesnake Point, Kelso and Mount Nemo provide some of the best rock-climbing, and certainly the best rock-climbing instruction areas in eastern North America. This locale has provided our family with countless recreational opportunities. Ryan and Keltie had their first climbing experiences at Rattlesnake, impressing first-time and experienced climbers with their confidence in both Dad and technology. They bounced from climb to climb suspended by a fabricated harness and climbing rope, occasionally standing on the shoulder of another understanding climber who thankfully saw the humour in the situation. The escarpment is also a place of mystery and discovery. When Star Wars first emerged on the entertainment scene, I was able to convince my young family that Yoda, the wise rain-forest-dwelling character, just might live at Mount Nemo. This led to hours of exploring and learning about the incredible flora and fauna of the area. Amid lush green, intricate ferns we discovered the entrances to spectacular crevice caves and ventured through them, enjoying their coolness on the hot, muggy days of summer. One day our family was sure that we caught a glimpse of Yoda sitting by a flickering candle in a craggy corner of the crevice we were exploring!

DAVE AND MARGIE MOORE, OUTDOOR EDUCATORS, ROCK-CLIMBING INSTRUCTORS AND ESCARPMENT EXPLORERS

Everyone connects with nature differently. Some delight in the solitary pleasures of hiking and birdwatching, while others pursue more adventurous sports, such as rock-climbing and spelunking. Underlying these pastimes is a curiosity about and instinctive attraction to the natural world. In the conservation lands of the Halton watershed the opportunities to explore nature seem endless. The sheer cliffs and crevice caves that characterize Rattlesnake Point make it a mecca for rock-climbers, spelunkers and naturalists. Kelso Conservation Area is an outdoor enthusiast's four-season paradise. Whether it's hiking, mountain biking, downhill skiing or sailboarding, adventure is readily accessible to thousands of Southern Ontario residents at this Niagara Escarpment park.

The Niagara Escarpment is a ridge of sedimentary rock that formed the outer rim of a shallow sea approximately 450 million years ago. Outliers, such as the one where Rattlesnake Point and Milton Heights are

Rock-climbing at Rattlesnake Point Conservation Area, Milton.
PAT AND ROSEMARIE KEOUGH

situated, are among the Niagara Escarpment's most prominent geological landmarks. An outlier is a part of the escarpment that is detached from the main section by a stream-eroded valley. Rattlesnake Point and Milton Heights at Kelso Conservation Area are part of the Milton Outlier, with Rattlesnake Point forming the southern tip and Milton Heights forming the northern end.

The legendary promontories of the Halton watershed are also home to the oldest and least-disturbed forest in all of eastern North America. This ancient forest was first discovered at Kelso, then at other escarpment areas such as Mount Nemo, where the watershed's oldest living white cedar, dated at 850 years, is located. Even more amazing is the recent discovery of a new habitat previously unknown on the escarpment. A community of microorganisms known as crytoendoliths live right inside escarpment rocks. Ecologist Doug Larson, who uncovered these natural wonders, has contributed greatly to our understanding of this fragile ecosystem.

The grandeur of Rattlesnake Point entices us to explore this promontory at a closer range. Rock-climbers at Rattlesnake Point test the strength of mind and body against the ancient escarpment face. With dolostone cliffs ranging from 10 to 30 metres in height, Rattlesnake Point is one of the best rock faces in Southern Ontario for recreational and instructional climbing. During the peak summer season, Rattlesnake Point, nicknamed "the beach," is inundated with climbers. There are more than forty recognized climbs or pitches here. Each pitch is rated on a decimal system from 5.0 to 5.14. Rattlesnake's first 5.11 climb, named "Space Case" or "The Way We Were," is an outstanding accomplishment for climbers on a rock face this size. At one time 5.9 was considered the human limit, but many of today's climbers easily accomplish 5.11 pitches.

With the growing popularity of rock-climbing, however, the fragile ecosystem of the cliff and its ancient cedars are under stress. Climbers must be conscious of this biologically sensitive ecosystem and adhere to an environmental ethic while climbing the crags. The Halton Region Conservation Authority has a comprehensive sustainability strategy to protect this important natural site.

While climbers defy acrophobia, spelunkers descend into claustrophobic caverns in the earth. The escarpment is a magnet for cave explorers. Most escarpment caves were formed during the retreat of the Wisconsin glaciers nearly 12,000 years ago. There are four basic types of limestone caves: crevice, sea, ice and solution. Crevice caves are the most

common, and both Rattlesnake Point and Mount Nemo have good examples. Crevice caves develop near the edge of the escarpment as joints. Cracks enlarge due to erosion, and the resistant dolostone caprock gradually breaks away. One cave at Rattlesnake Point is multilevelled and leads to a small chamber approximately 15 metres below ground.

In the microclimates of caves, removed from the sun, specialized species of plants and animals have evolved. The delicate flora and fauna are vulnerable to ecological damage. The eastern pipistrelle and small-footed bats, considered uncommon in Ontario, have been found in caves at Mount Nemo and Rattlesnake Point. If disturbed during hibernation, when their blood-sugar levels are reduced, bats can die from the sudden change in their metabolic rate. As with any human interaction with vulnerable ecosystems, precautions must be taken to protect the flora and fauna.

At the northern end of the Milton Outlier is the Kelso Conservation Area, an exceptional location for nature lovers and sports enthusiasts. During the summer, Kelso Lake teems with swimmers, fishing enthusiasts, canoeists and windsurfers. You may even find men and women testing their skills and stamina during gruelling triathlon events. In summer and fall, Kelso and Hilton Falls Conservation Areas have designated trails for off-road cycling. The spectacular Milton Heights promontory, with its 73-metre descent, provides some of the province's best mountain-biking trails, challenging novices and experts alike. The escarpment creates beautiful and thrilling terrain, from "sweet" single tracks to rocky technical sections. Cyclists using designated trails must abide by

Caving at Mount Nemo Conservation Area, Burlington.
NEIL HESTER

an ethical code to practise low-impact cycling, which includes avoiding wet areas, especially in spring, and not riding through streams.

By exchanging their mountain bikes for downhill skis or snowboards, outdoor adventurers can easily adjust to winter. The verdant cliffs of Kelso are transformed into Glen Eden, a recreational wonderland for downhill skiers and snowboarders. Twelve slopes of various terrain accommodate all skiing and boarding abilities. One quad chairlift, two triple lifts and one T-bar service 7,200 skiers per hour. Glen Eden also has extensive snowmaking capabilities and an excellent ski school.

In the conservation lands of the Halton watershed the opportunities to engage in outdoor adventure are limited only by imagination. A balance between preservation of natural areas and conscientious use will ensure their survival. The maxim "take only pictures, leave only footprints" will help protect Halton's magnificent promontories for future generations. In return, nature will continue to provide a haven from the stress of daily life.

MOUNTAIN BIKING AT KELSO CONSERVATION AREA, MILTON.
NEIL HESTER

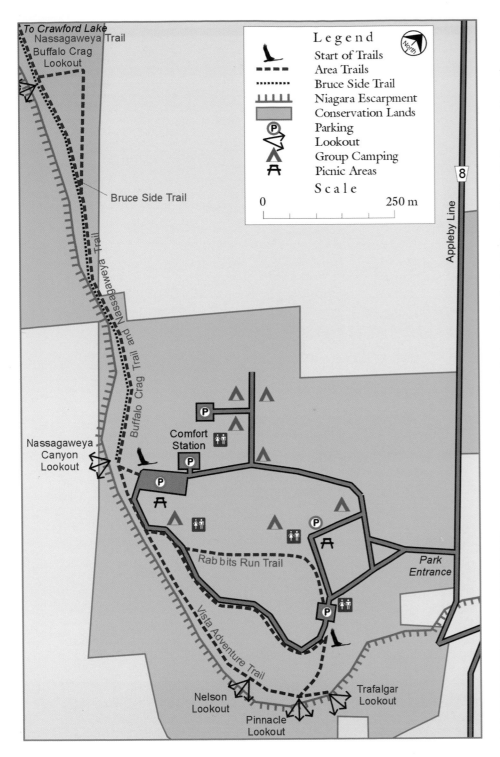

Legend

Start of Trails
Area Trails
Bruce Side Trail
Niagara Escarpment
Conservation Lands
Parking
Lookout
Group Camping
Picnic Areas

Scale

0   250 m

To Crawford Lake
Nassagaweya Trail
Buffalo Crag Lookout
Bruce Side Trail
Buffalo Crag Trail and Nassagaweya Trail
Nassagaweya Canyon Lookout
Comfort Station
Rabbits Run Trail
Park Entrance
Vista Adventure Trail
Nelson Lookout
Pinnacle Lookout
Trafalgar Lookout
Appleby Line
8

Watershed Guidepost
Rattlesnake Point Conservation Area, Milton

The mystique of outdoor adventure often takes people to the far corners of the globe. Yet all the components of a great adventure can be found in the Halton watershed at Rattlesnake Point Conservation Area. The majestic wildness of Rattlesnake Point, with its sheer cliffs and crevice caves, beckons to be explored. Even the name Rattlesnake Point is enigmatic — possibly a reference to a time when massasauga rattlesnakes were common in Halton Region.

A series of four loop trails, ranging in length from 1.5 to 5 kilometres, begins at the head of trails. Lookouts with spectacular views of the countryside, such as Trafalgar with a view of Lake Ontario and Toronto, and Nelson with a great look at the Lowville valley and Mount Nemo, are situated at five cliff-edge points along the trails. The trails can be completed as loops or you can take a longer hike on the Nassagaweya Trail, which connects Rattlesnake Point with Crawford Lake Conservation Area.

Rattlesnake Point is located in the transition zone between the Carolinian and Great Lakes–St. Lawrence Forest Zones. The conservation area has a diversity of plant species, such as burning bush and spice bush, which are usually associated with more southern climates, as well as numerous ferns and mosses that have adapted to this rugged landscape.

Whether you are a climber, caver or weekend recreationalist, Rattlesnake Point has an abundance of wildlife and adventure — all within close proximity to major urban areas.

Directions: From Highway 401, take Highway 25 north (Exit 320) to Campbellville Road, west to Tremaine Road, south to Steeles Avenue, west to Appleby Line, then turn south to the park entrance. From the QEW, take Highway 25 north (Exit 111) to Derry Road, west to Tremaine Road, north to Steeles Avenue, west to Appleby Line, then turn south to the park entrance.

Nature Calls - Turkey Vultures and Carrion Canyon

Listening to the wind whistle through the scenic Nassagaweya Canyon at Buffalo Crag Lookout is inspiring and relaxing. The site also yields other natural surprises. This is a great place to watch soaring turkey vultures looking for carrion and cliff-edge nesting sites. The birds use the thermal updrafts caused by air moving up the escarpment cliffs to remain airborne for hours. With wings forming the shape of a shallow V, the vultures can often be seen at eye level from the lofty perch of the lookout. Look for the small red head and the two-metre long black wings of these majestic fliers. The birds help keep the environment free of dead animals and can be seen between March and October.

Nelson Lookout at Rattlesnake Point Conservation Area, Milton. Neil Hester

A SAILBOARD GLIDES ACROSS KELSO LAKE WITH THE ESCARPMENT IN THE BACKGROUND, KELSO CONSERVATION AREA, MILTON. PAT AND ROSEMARIE KEOUGH

A GROOMING MACHINE PREPARES THE SLOPES FOR NIGHT SKIING, GLEN EDEN SKI AREA, MILTON. Neil Hester

A BIRD'S-EYE VIEW OF SCENIC GREYSTONE GOLF COURSE FROM ATOP NIAGARA ESCARPMENT, HALTON HILLS. NEIL HESTER

9

LIMESTONE LEGACY AND SCENIC LINKS
Exploring Halton Hills

The course of my life was shaped by family and agriculture, especially growing apples. My father, grandfather and great-grandfather all grew apples not far from our farm in Halton Hills. My father was the first grower in Canada to import dwarf rootstock from England and my grandfather was Ontario's Minister of Agriculture for almost forty years. Today agriculture is still an important activity in the Halton watershed and many farms have generous bits of nature intertwined with orchards, crops and livestock. Our farm, with twenty-eight thousand apple trees, has a spectacular backdrop, the Niagara Escarpment, which enhances the pick-your-own experience. Halton's seamless blend of conservation and farmlands make this area one of the best places to live, work and play anywhere, bar none.

TOM CHUDLEIGH, APPLE GROWER, CHUDLEIGH'S FARM

The history of Halton Hills is rooted in a land of soil, trees and rock, the abundant natural resources that first brought surveyors and then British settlers to this area in 1819. Halton Hills — formerly Esquesing Township and the towns of Georgetown and Acton — is rich in the natural and cultural resources of its rural past. The countryside maintains its rural character and continues to bear the mark of its early beginnings: scattered woodlots, picturesque farms and industrial remnants.

In the nineteenth century, industries based on wood, leather processing, papermaking, and mineral extraction flourished in Esquesing Township. The township was well situated to take advantage of cheap rail transportation. The Grand Trunk Railway (now Canadian National Railway) and the Hamilton & North Western line ran through the township. Located on the new railway network, Acton and Georgetown became the township's major urban centres.

Visitors wait for wagon rides to the apple orchard, Chudleigh's Farm, Halton Hills. GARY HUTTON

The Niagara Escarpment, dominating one-third of Halton Hills, attracted a fair share of industry to the area in the nineteenth century. The escarpment was a natural source of early construction material, including limestone, brick and tile, marble, sand and gravel. The lime-mortar industry used the dolostone from the escarpment to make plaster, mortar and whitewash. Dolostone is similar to limestone but more durable because of its high magnesium content. The village of Limehouse, known as Fountain Green until the post office opened in 1857, was the centre of Esquesing Township's lime-mortar production. Quantities of rock were heated in ovenlike structures called kilns. Early commercial kilns were simply hollows dug into the escarpment. By 1850 set kilns, a new technological innovation, had further refined the process. Set kilns, approximately 3 metres high, could hold 800 bushels of rock and would consume 20 cords of wood over three to four days. Progress continued with the introduction of draw or shaft kilns, which were approximately 16 metres high and could burn day and night. In the early twentieth century, Limehouse boasted ten kilns in full operation. The success of Limehouse also heralded its demise. Production costs soared when the local forest became depleted and the wood required for fuel had to be imported from other regions. Soon the larger, more modern kilns bought out the small operators. By 1918 the kilns at Limehouse were silent. The stone ruins remain to remind hikers and cross-country skiers of a different era.

The escarpment is still mined for its mineral resources. Since the Halton watershed is close to major urban centres and highways, the escarpment provides a substantial amount of aggregate for urban development and the expansion of our transportation infrastructure. The headwaters of the majority of streams in the watershed also rise from the escarpment. Careful planning for the extraction of aggregate must be carried out to minimize damage to the fragile network of these creeks and wetlands.

Quarry operators have responded with rehabilitation programs to restore the land in ways compatible with the surrounding landscape. In 1991 Dufferin Aggregates completed the first phase of a rehabilitation program at their quarry near the Esquesing Conservation Area. Also, with the co-operation of Dufferin Aggregates, the Bruce Trail Association and the Halton Region Conservation Authority, a bridge was erected across a gap in the escarpment, which relocated the Bruce Trail onto its optimum route. An interpretive display on quarrying and the Niagara Escarpment has been installed at the site.

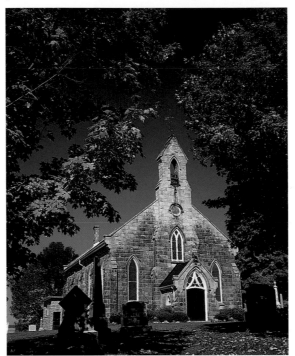

Boston Church, Mansewood, Halton Hills.
NEIL HESTER

An important program of the Halton Region Conservation Authority is the management of water resources in the Halton watershed, including water-quality issues and the protection of fragile wetland ecosystems. Escarpment wetlands have a direct impact on stream flows and also provide natural flood storage and recharge areas. Water resources are managed to prevent loss of life, and property damage from stream-bank erosion and flooding. Scotch Block Reservoir in Halton Hills is one of four water-control structures. The others are at Kelso, Hilton Falls and Mountsberg. These reservoirs store water during high flows in watershed creeks and augment water supplies during periods of low flow. Some of the conservation areas, such as Kelso and Mountsberg, have also developed recreational and educational programs that are complementary to the reservoirs.

Halton Hills has a range of recreational opportunities, from hiking and cross-country skiing at Esquesing Conservation Area, to golfing at many picturesque golf courses or horseback riding at an equestrian centre. Day-trippers can also experience the pleasures of farm life. Local farmers have developed pick-your-own operations and offer such rural amenities as wagon rides, baked goods and preserves. Tom and Carol Chudleigh operate one of the most successful pick-your-own farms in the area. The Chudleigh's slogan, "An Entertaining Taste of the Country," epitomizes this new approach to agriculture. Visitors to the pick-your-own farms enjoy the sights, sounds and smells of a great day in the country.

HISTORIC LIME KILNS AT LIMEHOUSE CONSERVATION AREA, HALTON HILLS. NEIL HESTER

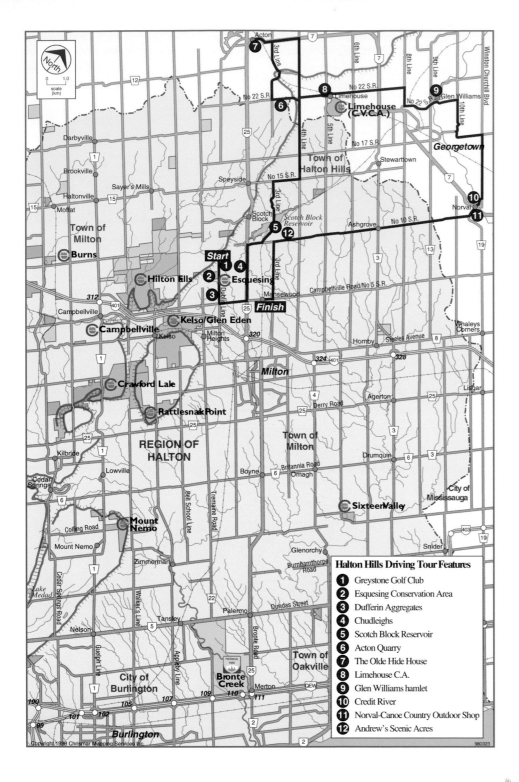

Halton Hills Driving Tour Features

1. Greystone Golf Club
2. Esquesing Conservation Area
3. Dufferin Aggregates
4. Chudleighs
5. Scotch Block Reservoir
6. Acton Quarry
7. The Olde Hide House
8. Limehouse C.A.
9. Glen Williams hamlet
10. Credit River
11. Norval-Canoe Country Outdoor Shop
12. Andrew's Scenic Acres

Watershed Guidepost
Halton Hills Driving Tour

A driving tour along the backroads of Halton Hills is a great way to experience the diversity of the area firsthand. This 60-kilometre driving tour begins on Dublin Line in the southwest corner of Halton Hills. As you go north on this dead-end road, you can view the Niagara Escarpment as it begins its bulking diagonal division of Halton Hills. This 2-kilometre initial stretch dramatically shows the many uses of escarpment lands. The entrance to Dufferin Quarry is on the left, where you can see the Bruce Trail bridge that crosses a gap in the escarpment created by quarry operations. A short distance further along you reach the rich woods of the Esquesing Conservation Area, followed by the beautiful, lush green Greystone golf course that brushes the escarpment's talus slopes.

From here the tour heads north to Chudleigh's apple farm and then over a causeway at the Scotch Block water-control reservoir. At the edge of the watershed, you go up and down the escarpment, past the Acton Quarry and into Acton. From this point, you enter the neighbouring Credit River watershed through the charming communities of Limehouse, Glen Williams and Norval. A short hike on the Bruce Trail at Limehouse reveals intriguing lime-kiln ruins and dramatic limestone fissures. The driving tour ends through rich agricultural lands complete with several excellent pick-your-own farms. The ninety-minute drive takes much longer if you stop and linger at the sites along the way.

Directions: From Highway 401, take Highway 25 north (Exit 320) to Campbellville Road, and turn west to Dublin Line and north to the start of the driving tour. From the QEW, take Highway 25 north (Exit 111) through Milton to Campbellville Road, than turn west to Dublin Line and north to the start of the driving tour.

Nature Calls - Butterflies and Bluejays

Pick-your-own farms are often as much fun and as delightfully colourful as their products are tasty. With a bounty of richly hued fruits, acres of dancing blossoms and a nearly endless parade of greenery, the farmscape is also a great place to experience nature. Listen for the sounds of children having fun — on hay bales, in fields of colourful flowers, and among rows of sunflowers higher than they are. These are also great spots to see monarch, black swallowtail and viceroy butterflies flitter and flutter among the blossoms in search of nectar. Watch, too, for migrating bluejays belting out their *jay, jay* cries as they touch down on sunflower landing pads.

ROBERT McCAW

PICK-YOUR-OWN FLOWERS AND HAY BALE FUN, ANDREW'S SCENIC ACRES, HALTON HILLS. GARY HUTTON

CYCLING ON A COUNTRY ROAD IN THE FALL, HALTON HILLS. NEIL HESTER

The limestone and cedar artistry of the Niagara Escarpment near Limehouse, Halton Hills. Neil Hester

MILTON HEIGHTS SUNRISE, KELSO CONSERVATION AREA, MILTON. NEIL HESTER

10

COUNTRY ROADS AND RURAL ROOTS: Exploring Milton

Milton has an abundance of less travelled roads that are fun to explore and an inspiration to experience. I love turning out my driveway with no destination in mind, letting chance roll the dice at every intersection. The treasures you find will surprise you — a cathedral of brilliant maples, a snake-rail fence, or a forgotten village with a quaint general store that has great ice cream. For me these sites and scenes often create story ideas, hidden in the guise of a great day in the country. Milton also has many pioneer churches and cemeteries that conjure up daydreams of our forebearers walking this area for the first time. The brief inscriptions on the weathered tombstones speak volumes about hardship and courage and love — so many short lives, so many young mothers and children left forever in youth but held in hearts, literally, to the grave. Still, the pretty and peaceful surroundings suggest that for those early immigrants, this was a place they called home. Do you remember printing your first S? That's the kind of road I'm looking for, something convoluted that defies Ontario's prosaic grid, an old gravel road that twists and turns like a snake sliding into the creek for a drink. There is nothing quite like cresting a deserted hill and finding yourself in a forgotten village, or suddenly discovering a small, vibrant community, such as Campbellville, where you can explore the antique and craft shops or just relax by the pond in the Campbellville Conservation Area. I also like forbidden driveways — catching a glimpse of a stately stone house through the trees, or a log house nestled beside a silver-green pond, looking, to the outsider, like some perfect, self-enclosed universe. How do you find these side roads to adventure? Avoid asphalt. Asphalt speaks of civilization and we're looking for neglect. Always take the road with a sign that says, "No winter maintenance beyond this point." Robert Frost said it best: "Two roads diverged in a yellow wood . . . And I, I took the one less traveled by/ And that has made all the difference."

JOHN DENISON, PUBLISHER, BOSTON MILLS PRESS

Commuters whizzing along Highway 401 near Milton may recognize the familiar landmark of Milton Heights but often have little time to appreciate its beauty. The pace, however, slows on the backroads of Milton. There is time to observe and time to contemplate the subtle details of the countryside.

The Halton Region Museum and Kelso Conservation Area, nestled at the foot of Milton Heights, are both situated on the former Alexander family farm. In 1961 Adam Alexander IV, the fourth generation to farm this 81 hectares of land, sold the property to the Sixteen Mile Creek Conservation Authority for water control and recreation. A notable family member was Adam Alexander III, who harnessed the power of a stream running over the Niagara Escarpment and generated enough electricity for his house and his farm machinery. Adam III was ahead of his contemporaries who still used kerosene lighting and horse-

Historic Christie-Henderson lime kilns, Kelso Conservation Area, Milton. ALAN ERNST

powered machinery. The Alexander family house and barn, and other original nineteenth-century structures, have been incorporated into the facilities of the Halton Region Museum. Part of the museum's collection is an exceptional exhibit that spans 12,000 years of Halton's natural and cultural history.

Within Kelso Conservation Area are the Christie-Henderson lime kilns, considered the best-preserved lime kilns in Ontario. In the nineteenth century, the lime-mortar industry was vital to the growth of early towns, and the nearby escarpment provided the requisite limestone. Commercial lime was used in the building industry, in the manufacture of glass, and as a disinfectant. The Christie-Henderson lime kilns were built in the 1880s and ceased operation in 1929.

The Farm Museum, formerly the Ontario Agricultural Museum, is a short drive down the road from Kelso

Conservation Area. Costumed interpreters delight schoolchildren and adults as they perform tasks from pioneer life using authentic tools and methods. The museum is well known for its contemporary and traditional quilt collection. There are over thirty buildings to explore on the 32-hectare site.

At the centre of "Escarpment Country" is the Town of Milton. This community, which straddles the meandering Sixteen Mile Creek, has drawn people to its banks since 1822, when Jasper Martin established a gristmill along the creek. In the early days, farmers would walk 19 to 24 kilometres to mill their wheat at Martin's Mill. In 1836 George Brown officially opened a post office. As postmaster, Brown had the privilege of choosing the name for the community. Some residents believe the name was derived from "mill town," while others suggest that Milton was chosen in honour of the English poet John Milton.

In 1864 Milton council accepted the offer of Joseph Martin, the son of Jasper Martin, to provide the site for a new town hall. Martin proposed to build it for $5,000, and in 1866 the town hall was finished. It was an impressive building worthy of the town's political prominence in the county. Today Milton's turn-of-the-century architecture, treelined streets, historic millpond and magnificent town hall (a restored former county courthouse and jail) charm visitors.

Cars and highways may dominate today's landscape, but Canadians have always had a love affair with trains. In the 1850s Ontario's railway network was expanding and towns competed fiercely for the new rail service. With a population of 891 people, Milton voted to pay a bonus of $30,000 for the construction of the Credit Valley Railway, which ensured Milton's position on the new rail network.

Travelling back to yesteryear
at the Farm Museum, Milton. NEIL HESTER

To this day, Milton maintains a link with the heyday of the railways. Located in northern Milton is the Halton County Railway Museum, where people can still experience the thrill of riding a turn-of-the-century streetcar. The museum features classic antique electric-rail vehicles operating on 2 kilometres of scenic track. Also on-site is the Rockwood Station, built in 1912 for the Grand Trunk Railway. It was destined for demolition but was relocated from Rockwood to the railway museum in 1971.

The lush agricultural lands surrounding Milton provide a rich harvest of fruits and vegetables. Milton has a long agricultural tradition dating back to 1853 when the Halton Agricultural Society was organized and an annual fair was first held in Milton. Today a farmers' market is held every Saturday morning from June to October, on Main Street, in the heart of downtown, bringing vendors, residents and visitors together in a friendly community ritual.

Milton is also known for its abundance of nature. From the rich valleys of Sixteen Mile Creek to the spectacular cliffs of the Niagara Escarpment, Milton has one of the largest accumulations of conservation lands in urban Ontario. This natural landscape also includes a wide selection of challenging golf courses and a higher density of horses per acre than the state of Kentucky. In addition to harness racing at Mohawk, there are many standardbred and thoroughbred breeding facilities.

Nearby, the historic hamlets of Brookville, Moffat and Campbellville harmonize with the natural environment to produce a charming blend of nature and culture. The backroads that crisscross the escarpment in Milton are a breathtaking experience in themselves. Down these roads and in local museums are vestiges of Ontario's rural past that shaped our cultural legacy.

Six-hitch competition, Milton Fall Fair. Gary Hutton

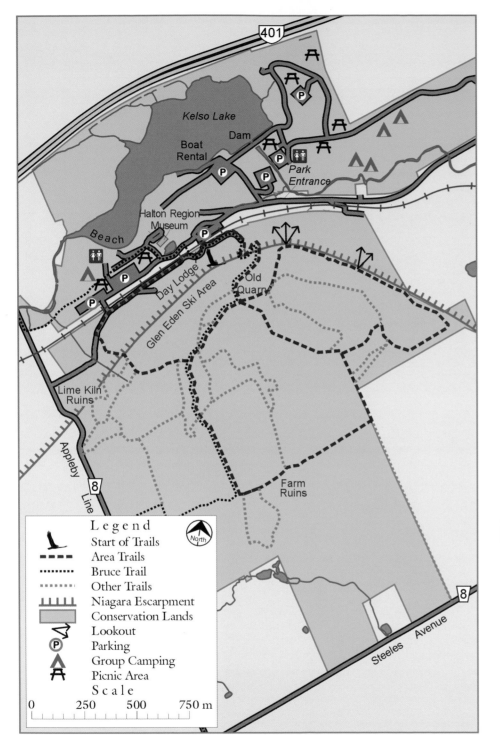

Legend

- Start of Trails
- Area Trails
- Bruce Trail
- Other Trails
- Niagara Escarpment
- Conservation Lands
- Lookout
- P Parking
- Group Camping
- Picnic Area

Scale

0   250   500   750 m

Watershed Guidepost
Kelso Conservation Area, Milton

The imposing cliffs of Milton Heights are a beacon for travellers along the highway. For recreation seekers, these same cliffs signal something more — a day of outdoor adventure, regardless of season, at Kelso Conservation Area. Sharing the same slopes of the escarpment are mountain bikers and hikers during summer and fall, and skiers and snowboarders in winter.

The hiking trails combine spectacular scenery of the countryside with cultural heritage, including the Christie-Henderson lime kilns, an old quarry and the Halton Region Museum. Kelso also has some of the most challenging mountain-biking trails in the province. These trails are designed with the thrill of mountain biking in mind. Many of the trails are technically challenging and have names like Grunt Climb, Rocky Downhill and Hawthorn Run. It is not unusual on a fall day to see the parking lot filled with cars sporting bike racks.

In winter, skiers take over the slopes at the Glen Eden Ski Area, which is located within Kelso. Glen Eden is fast becoming one of Ontario's leading urban ski and snowboarding areas. With a 73-metre vertical drop, snowmaking capabilities, a quad chairlift, two triple chairlifts and a new snowboarding park, Glen Eden proves a popular skiing destination. The whole family can enjoy the activities at Kelso Conservation Area — a truly year-round experience for fun and adventure.

Directions: From Highway 401, take Highway 25 north (Exit 320) to Campbellville Road, west to Tremaine Road, south to Kelso Road, then turn west to park entrance. From the QEW, take Highway 25 north (Exit 111) to Derry Road, west to Tremaine Road, north to Kelso Road, then turn west to park entrance.

Nature Calls – White-Breasted Nuthatch

As you scale the hills of Glen Eden for that spectacular view, watch for a bird clinging upside-down to large trees. This is the white-breasted nuthatch, and it is looking for insects in the ridges of bark on maple, oak and beech trees. Listen for *ank ank*, its familiar, woodsy call that broadcasts the nuthatch's presence to the world. This agile, daring flier has a black cap, white cheeks and breast, and a long bill to open the hatch in seeds such as acorns. When you reach the summit, look down on the Halton countryside as viewed from the upside-down perspective of the white-breasted nuthatch.

ROBERT McCAW

Kelso Conservation Area, Milton. Rob Stimpson

Inset: Flamboro Antique Show, Kelso Conservation Area, Milton. Conservation Halton

THE HEADWATERS OF SIXTEEN MILE CREEK FORM PONDS THROUGHOUT THE HISTORIC VILLAGE OF CAMPBELLVILLE. GEOFF GRENVILLE

Fishing on Golden Pond at the Millpond, Milton. Neil Hester

BRONTE HARBOUR, OAKVILLE. GEOFF GRENVILLE

SECRET GARDENS AND NATURAL SPACES: Exploring Oakville

I have always enjoyed nature, especially hiking, and photographing nature. Apart from the Bruce Trail and the exquisite conservation areas on the Niagara Escarpment, one of my favourite places in Halton is Oakville's Erchless Estate, with its beautiful gardens and lake vistas. Strolling along the carriage path that weaves through hundred-year-old trees by the lakeview gardens, I am reminded of the unique balance between nature and humans that is very much alive and respected in this modern town. From the years I spent researching, writing and photographing this harbour town for The Oakville Book, I have gained an understanding of the town's historical figures and the natural and man-made changes to the community. Oakville's incredible natural landscapes include two picturesque harbours, several creeks, extensive parkland, a waterfront trail, beaches, woodlots, ravines, hiking trails, gardens, farmland, a provincial park and countless old trees. In harmony with its natural spaces, Oakville has built a rich architectural heritage that is evident everywhere, from the nineteenth-century stores on Lakeshore Road to the limestone granary on Sixteen Mile Creek. This historic town has over a hundred designated heritage buildings. Oakville was first developed here because of its harbour and its natural resources. Today people still enjoy living in and visiting Oakville for the same reasons.

SHEILA CREIGHTON, WRITER AND PHOTOGRAPHER

The charming, historic Town of Oakville thrives at the mouth of Sixteen Mile Creek on the Lake Ontario shoreline where a natural harbour and prodigious forest of white pine and oak once flourished. On his journeys from Burlington to York in the 1820s, William Chisholm, an enterprising merchant and shipbuilder, recognized the commercial potential of Sixteen Mile Creek and the forest surrounding it. Chisholm was not the first person drawn to the banks of this creek. The Mississauga had farmed, hunted and fished at the mouth of Nassagaweya Creek since the 1700s. The development of Oakville, however, was the vision of William Chisholm.

Although many settlements bear the stamp of their early entrepreneurs, William Chisholm was involved in all aspects of Oakville's development; even the name "Oakville" is possibly derived from William's nickname, "White Oak." In 1827 William purchased 388 hectares at the mouth of Sixteen Mile Creek. He moved his

Erchless Estate, Oakville.
SHEILAH CREIGHTON

shipbuilding business from Burlington to Sixteen Mile Creek and constructed a sawmill, gristmill, warehouses and a harbour. At different times, William served as postmaster, justice of the peace, coroner, issuer of marriage licences, and collector of customs. His family continued his legacy of community involvement, George King Chisholm was the first mayor of Oakville, and William Chisholm's other sons and grandsons headed the community's industries.

Oakville's earliest export was lumber, especially white pine and oak. White pine as tall as 26 metres were used as ships' masts. As settlement spread inland and more forests were cleared for agriculture, grain replaced lumber as a major export. Between 1836 and 1860, Oakville was Halton's largest shipping and urban centre.

The mid-nineteenth century saw the dawn of an expanded railway network, and with it the cheap and reliable transportation of goods and people. The geographical location of the railway lines often made or ruined a community's future prosperity. When the new railway lines by-passed the lakeshore ports, it heralded the end of Oakville's days as a commercial harbour. Shipbuilding, however, continued in Oakville, with yacht construction replacing the construction of commercial ships.

Despite the growth of manufacturing centres in the hinterland, Oakville's economy was resilient. In the late nineteenth century, Oakville became a leading strawberry-producing area. With the focus on market gardens, fruits and vegetables, a basket- and barrel-making industry evolved. The Oakville Basket Company, later named Oakville Wood Specialists, operated from the 1860s to 1988.

Today Oakville is well known for its historic sites, exquisite mansions, art galleries and charming downtown. Many of its historic buildings reflect the influence of the Chisholm family. Romain House, George's Square, the Custom House, and Erchless Estate are all associated with the Chisholms. Five generations of the Chisholm family lived on the Erchless Estate. Erchless, which in Gaelic means "on the stream," recalls the family's clan seat and castle in Scotland. Robert Kerr Chisholm completed the mansion in 1858, and the Town of Oakville purchased the estate in 1976. It was authentically restored to the 1920 period, when Emelda Beeler Chisholm owned the property. The Oakville Museum and the Oakville Historical Society are located on the estate.

At the mouth of Morrison Creek is Gairloch Gardens, which includes a mansion built by Colonel MacKendrick after World War I. James Gairdner, a wealthy stockbroker and artist, purchased the house in 1960

Joshua's Creek Trail, Oakville.
Scott Robertson

and renamed it Gairloch, which means "short lake" in Gaelic. In his will, he bequeathed the estate to the Town of Oakville, and Gairloch is now an art gallery and a magnificent park.

At the turn of the century, Oakville was known as "Toronto's summer playground." Its environs are still associated with sports and recreation, especially golf. Since 1977 Glen Abbey Golf Club, which was designed by Jack Nicklaus, has hosted the Canadian Open Golf Tournament since 1977. It attracts professional golfers from around the world and sometimes over 100,000 spectators. Glen Abbey also houses the Royal Canadian Golf Association Museum and the Canadian Golf Hall of Fame.

Horse breeding and equestrian sports are also well established in the Oakville area. In 1860 the thoroughbred Don Juan from Merton won the first Queen's Plate. Carrying on the tradition of excellence are a variety of breeding and show-jumping facilities located throughout Oakville.

Oakville also has an extensive park and trail system, including Iroquois Shoreline Woods, Lakeside Park, Morrison Creek Trail, Shipyard Park, and Joshua's Creek Trail. Iroquois Shoreline Woods is the largest in the Oakville parks system. The distinctive terrace that runs diagonally across the property was formed by glacial Lake Iroquois, a larger ancestor of Lake Ontario. Lake Iroquois was formed 10,000 years ago as the Wisconsin ice sheet receded from Southern Ontario. The woodlot is the largest upland oak-maple forest remaining below the Niagara Escarpment. Wood ducks, eastern screech owls, Nashville warblers and great horned owls are found in the woodlot. A series of loop trails allows visitors to explore the area's significant natural features.

PLEASURE BOATING IS A POPULAR SUMMER PASTIME AT OAKVILLE HARBOUR. SCOTT ROBERTSON

The Joshua's Creek Trail winds through Joshua Valley Park. Joshua's Creek is named after Joshua Leach, who purchased the land in 1822 and built a sawmill and house. The land was quickly harvested for its white pine and oak. Thomas Smith, an Oakville lumber dealer who owned the adjacent land, cut 2,000,000 board feet of pine from 10 hectares in 1848. Today black walnut, green ash and willow are reclaiming the land and concealing the remains of Leach's sawmill.

Nearly two centuries later, after William Chisholm envisioned his settlement, Oakville has expanded to a population of 127,000 people. The Town of Oakville includes the villages of Bronte, Palermo and Sheridan. William Chisholm might not recognize his natural harbour, but his entrepreneurial spirit certainly would be proud of well-preserved yet modern Oakville.

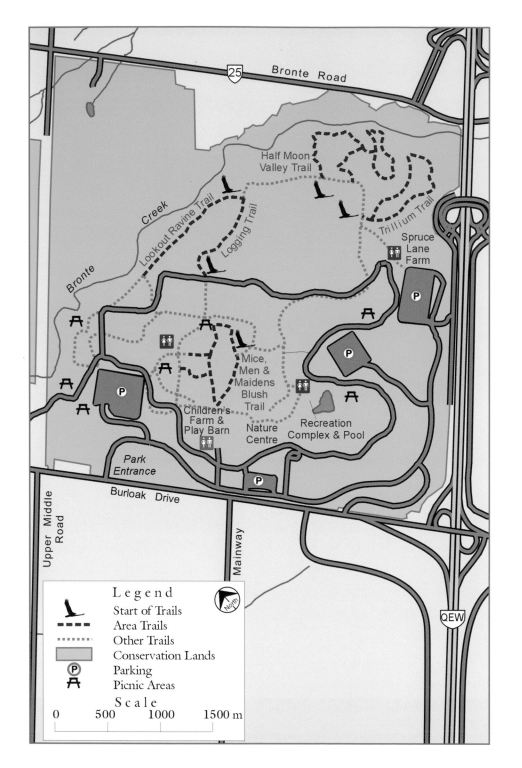

Watershed Guidepost
Bronte Creek Provincial Park, Oakville

Only a short distance from the charming Town of Oakville is Bronte Creek Provincial Park. Bronte Creek cuts a deep, narrow gorge through the park that provides a sanctuary for many unusual plants and animals. It is a spectacular place to observe nature, whether your interest is wildflowers, songbirds, or butterflies.

Several historic farms within the 640-hectare park have been converted into museums and provide a cultural context for the area. Self-guided interpretive trails provide insightful information on the natural heritage of Bronte Creek. Walk through the Buckholder Woods on the Mice, Men and Maiden's Blush Trail or witness wildflowers growing unabashedly in the forest of the Trillium Trail. The Half-Moon Valley Trail winds through the creek valley and features the park's most spectacular scenery. Local legend asserts that a Mississauga chief's white stallion can still be seen galloping through the valley on misty summer mornings.

Bronte Creek Provincial Park has all the ingredients for a successful family outing — swimming, hiking, picnicking, cross-country skiing and cycling. What better retreat from the chaos of urban life exists so close to home?

Directions: From the QEW, take Burloak Drive north (Exit 109) to the park entrance on the east side of road.

Nature Calls –
Warbling Bluebirds in a Box

 The Halton watershed is still graced with a few good bluebird haunts, one of which is Bronte Creek Provincial Park. A renowned harbinger of spring, the bluebird was once as common as the robin but now is a real treat to see. During migration bluebirds usually arrive before robins and sometimes are spotted in late snowstorms in March. Look for bluebirds in open woods, fields of second growth and old orchards. They nest in cavities in trees or posts, as well as in the man-made nesting boxes that have greatly benefitted the species. These shy blue birds with distinctive orange breasts welcome spring with their rich-toned *cheerily, cheerily* song. Famous naturalist Henry David Thoreau once said, "If the warble of the first bluebird does not thrill you, know that the morning and spring of your life are past."

TRILLIUM TRAIL, BRONTE CREEK PROVINCIAL PARK, OAKVILLE. ALAN ERNST

Inset: AN ARTIST AMONG THE TRILLIUMS, BRONTE CREEK PROVINCIAL PARK. ROB STIMPSON

Trail over Sixteen Mile Creek, Lions Valley Park, Oakville. Rob Boak

Inset: Erchless Estate gardens near Fisherman's Wharf Park, Oakville. Maggie Mills

SIXTEEN MILE CREEK MEANDERS THROUGH GLEN ABBEY GOLF COURSE, OAKVILLE.   GEOFF GRENVILLE

WILD AND GREEN MOUNT NEMO CONSERVATION AREA RISES BEHIND A PAIR OF CURIOUS HORSES, BURLINGTON. NEIL HESTER

12

MOUNT NEMO MAGIC AND INSPIRING WATERWAYS
Exploring Burlington

The course of my life was framed by the geology and ecology of the Burlington area. As a child, I lived right on the shore of Burlington Bay. My bedroom was only 30 metres from the water's edge. With a small canoe, I explored the bay, the marshes and the mouths of the creeks. Often I rambled ashore to climb the bluffs to the west of La Salle Park. My grandparents are buried at the bluffs' edge, their resting place still protected from erosion by the huge trees firmly rooted into the cliff. I walked to school though a narrow valley that in spring was a golden riot of marsh marigolds. At that season, the tiny creek teemed with spawning suckers. Some days I became so absorbed in their antics that, inadvertently, I ended up playing hooky. When not too distracted, I climbed out of the hardwoods onto the flats to walk the final mile. There the cherry and peach orchards and the market gardens formed an agricultural landscape that were unlike the cool, dark valleys I had left behind. As I grew older, much of what I knew then was lost. The bay became polluted and sick. Farms were subdivided, paved over or sprouted office complexes. Valleys were bulldozed and orchards and woods cut down. From this loss was born the longing that has dominated my work to restore the land and to protect the waters. Now, because of conservation efforts in the Halton watershed, the land is being protected and the waters are being given the deep respect they deserve. There has been a change in consciousness and, with it, a sense of hope. Once again we honour the land, the water and the creatures that inhabit our bioregion. We are coming to know that to be truly alive one must become a steward.

DR. JOHN TODD, PRESIDENT, OCEAN ARC INTERNATIONAL, MASSACHUSETTS

Mount Nemo rises majestically above Burlington. From a lookout perched atop its 23-metre-high limestone cliffs, the CN Tower is visible in the distance. Below is a valley of fertile farmland and spring-fed creeks. Burlington, with a foot in each world, embraces the best of city and country.

Burlington has a vast number of natural places to explore within the city and in the surrounding countryside. Opportunities to hike the Bruce Trail, walk through the Royal Botanical Gardens, and visit the conservation lands of the Halton watershed have made residents sensitive to environmental concerns. Often places such as Mount Nemo have left indelible memories on local residents and fostered a strong stewardship ethic.

"Sometimes in colder weather or on holidays, I would seek the high ground away from the bay, passing through groves of apple trees until I reached the clay pits. The red

Hiking along the Niagara Escarpment through Grindstone Creek valley, Burlington.
BRENDA AXON

earth, abandoned kilns, small railway cars and bricks still there bore witness to a once thriving local industry. Higher up were springs filled with watercress that never froze. Deer often came there to drink. In deep hardwood groves up under the escarpment, I discovered mysterious limestone caves and outcroppings. The views went on forever. The caves were cool in summer — and scary. I felt the presence of bygone peoples, the earlier inhabitants of those same retreats and perches. In that place I felt, for the first time, the integration of mindscape and landscape. The earth became home to me," writes Dr. John Todd.

Travel along the backroads of Burlington and discover scenic spots that inspire awe and reaffirm a connection with this place called home. Historic Lowville is a charming stopover on Burlington's country roads. Lowville Park, on the banks of Bronte Creek, has been a favourite recreation site for fifty years. The park boasted the first illuminated rural baseball field in Ontario. It is an ideal location for family picnics, baseball tournaments, and tobogganing in the winter.

Lake Medad is another familiar landmark. It is the only naturally occurring lake in the Grindstone Creek watershed. This spring-fed lake is unusual because it has no known outlet. It has a relatively stable depth of 24 metres and the bottom 18 metres are a suspended layer of murky ooze. The heavily forested Medad Valley and its provincially significant wetlands provide extensive habitats for numerous species of flora and fauna. The lake, named after the settler Medad Parson, is also archaeologically significant. In the 1980s archaeologists found aboriginal artifacts from the Neutral settlement of Kandoucho near the lake. In the 1640s the Jesuits visited this settlement, making specific reference to it on their maps. Snake Road, originally a Native footpath, is thought to have connected Kandoucho to Burlington Bay.

The City of Burlington is home to the world-renowned Royal Botanical Gardens. The site was created in the 1940s to conserve plants and natural habitats for people to enjoy. Today the 1,094 hectares of nature sanctuary and gardens have cool woodlands, wildflower meadows, escarpment cliffs, streams and marshes. The Royal Botanical Gardens is involved with many conservation programs such as marsh restoration in Cootes Paradise and Grindstone Creek marshes, two significant natural areas located at the western edge of the Halton watershed.

Along the Lake Ontario waterfront, there is an abundance of green

Niagara Escarpment in blaze of fall colours, Kerncliff Park, Burlington.

SANDY BELL

space — La Salle, Spencer Smith, Sioux Lookout, and McNichol Parks. La Salle Park marks the place where the French explorer Sieur de La Salle landed in 1669. The enchanting pavilion, originally built in 1917, that graces La Salle Park was once a popular venue for summer dances. The pavilion was recently destroyed by fire but was rebuilt to its original glory and is now used as a community centre.

While these backroads and parks soothe the spirit, Burlington's downtown is filled with historic buildings and museums to inspire the mind. A walking tour along the older streets of Burlington will reveal many cultural landmarks. Downtown Burlington, originally Wellington Square, was part of a land grant known as Brant's Block. Joseph Brant, born Thayendanegea, was a leader of the Six Nations and is considered one of Burlington's founding fathers. In 1778 the British granted Brant 1,397 hectares for his loyalty during the American Revolution. Today the Brant House Museum, a two-storey Regency-style reconstruction of Brant's original house overlooks the lake.

Early farmers prospered in the Burlington area because of the fertile soil and moderate temperatures. As more settlers arrived and cleared the land, cash crops replaced subsistence farming. Gradually, mixed farming and market gardens became the dominant form of agriculture, and in the early twentieth century the area was declared the "Garden of Canada." The first peaches grown in Canada were cultivated in the Grindstone Creek watershed. This farming tradition has passed down through the generations. Today over forty percent of the Grindstone Creek watershed is still devoted to farms, orchards and nurseries.

Naturally, a community flourishing in the shadow of Mount Nemo and having all these green spaces has a tradition of conservation. Over thirty years ago, the Halton Region Conservation Authority acquired 35 hectares to protect Mount Nemo from a quarry operation that proposed breaking through the face of the cliff. In response to public concern, a provincial committee studied the ecological significance of the Niagara Escarpment. This ultimately led to the development of a protection plan for the escarpment in 1985. Burlington is also home to the Canada Centre for Inland Waters, one of the world's leading freshwater research facilities. Thanks to the conservation of Mount Nemo and creek ecosystems, one can still find in Burlington's surroundings a calming retreat from urban life. The restoration of the waterfront and lands within the Royal Botanical Gardens ensures that future generations will continue to enjoy the diversity of natural experiences that are available in Burlington.

Rich farmland and scenic golf courses provide a great view from atop Mount Nemo, Burlington. Neil Hester

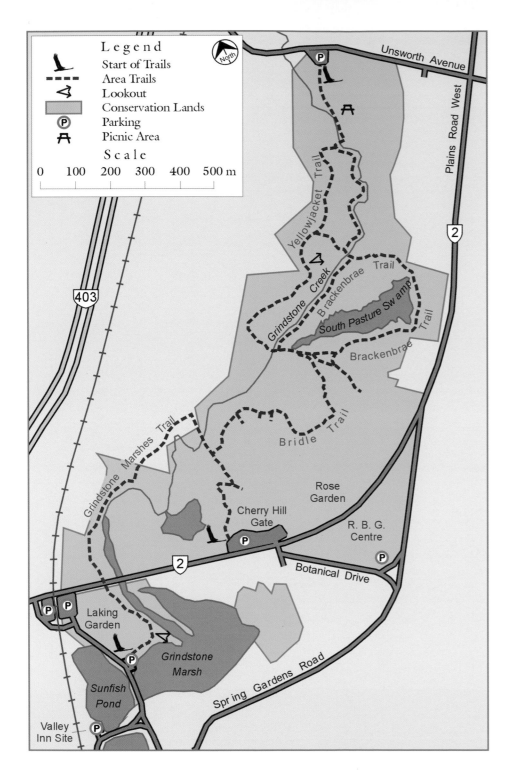

Legend

- Start of Trails
- Area Trails
- Lookout
- Conservation Lands
- Parking
- Picnic Area

Scale

0   100   200   300   400   500 m

North

Unsworth Avenue

Plains Road West

Yellowjacket Trail

Grindstone Creek

Brackenbrae Trail

South Pasture Swamp

Brackenbrae Trail

Grindstone Marshes Trail

Bridle Trail

Cherry Hill Gate

Rose Garden

R. B. G. Centre

Botanical Drive

Laking Garden

Grindstone Marsh

Sunfish Pond

Spring Gardens Road

Valley Inn Site

Watershed Guidepost

Hendrie Valley Trails, Royal Botanical Gardens, Burlington

Away from the industrial heartland of Hamilton, across Burlington Bay, are the Royal Botanical Gardens, an oasis of cultivated gardens, natural wetlands and untamed wilderness. This living museum is home to rare Carolinian species, the world's largest lilac collection, a spectacular rose garden and over 30 kilometres of hiking trails. Grindstone Creek valley, which runs through the Hendrie Valley Sanctuary, is an important part of the Royal Botanical Gardens and it is a natural wildlife corridor linking the escarpment and Burlington Bay. The Hendrie Valley Sanctuary has over 103 hectares of marsh, streams and wooded slopes. Named after William Hendrie, a prominent local philanthropist, the Hendrie Valley Sanctuary has a significant natural and cultural heritage.

As you hike the trails of the Hendrie Valley, compare the habitats of the creek valley — the wetlands in the lower reaches and the meadow community in the upper flood plain. These habitats include wildlife species such as blue-grey gnatcatchers, wood ducks, painted turtles and unusual plants such as silverrod and low sweet blueberry.

The Grindstone Creek valley, pike spawning marshes and Cootes Paradise marsh restoration are part of the Hamilton Harbour Fish and Wildlife Restoration Project. Cootes Paradise was once described as an "earthly paradise" but a century of industrial pollution, land filling, and the elimination of marshes destroyed this pristine habitat. The Cootes Paradise project is attempting to return life to the water. As you hike the trails, watch for interpretive plaques throughout the sanctuary describing the wetlands, flood abatement and water filtration methods, and the relationships between the creek, the harbour and Lake Ontario environments.

Directions: Follow the highway signs for Royal Botanical Gardens Centre from Highways 403, 6 or 2 (York Boulevard from Hamilton, Plains Road west from Burlington). Park at Cherry Hill Gate west of the Rose Garden, or walk from the RBG Centre through the Rose Garden.

Nature Calls - Fish Runs and Wood Ducks

A leisurely stroll along the Grindstone Marshes Trail reveals many natural surprises. You often hear more critters than you see. During spring listen for the *splish splash* of pike as they swim upstream to spawn in controlled wetlands that ensure the young pikes' return to the bay. In late fall, watch for Chinook and coho salmon and brown trout moving up Grindstone Creek to spawn. Listen, too, for the wood duck, one of nature's most colourful birds. The iridescent blue-green male with red eyes and beak has a haunting *whooeek, whooeek* call as it heads for cover.

ROBERT McCAW

Cyclists pause at the bridge along Grindstone Marshes Trail, Royal Botanical Gardens, Burlington. Jeff Marko

Spring gardens in full bloom at Royal Botanical Gardens, Burlington. Neil Hester

A FREIGHTER PASSES THROUGH THE BURLINGTON CANAL NEAR THE HISTORIC BURLINGTON BAY LIGHTHOUSE. MARK ZELINSKI

A SPECTACULAR SUNRISE ALONG THE WATERFRONT FROM BAYSHORE WINDOW-ON-THE-LAKE, BURLINGTON. SANDY BELL

13

ALONG THE SHORE OF LAKE ONTARIO: The Waterfront Trail

For some time, the significance of waterfronts was lost and their importance diminished; the great contribution of our river valleys was no longer understood or taught, and save for a few hardy souls, the essential role of nature in the city was all but forgotten. But this is changing. From Barcelona to Boston, from Halifax to Vancouver, from Shanghai to Toronto, reawakened waterfronts are being reclaimed by their cities and, in the process, both are being transformed in form, function and image. Along the shore of Lake Ontario, the Waterfront Trail is helping us rediscover the meaning of waterfronts — economically, historically and spiritually.

DAVID CROMBIE, CHAIR, WATERFRONT REGENERATION TRUST

The Waterfront Trail does more than just link existing trails and parklands along the Lake Ontario shoreline — it also serves as a symbol of communities reconnecting with their waterfronts. Waterfront communities are rediscovering the shoreline. By way of the Waterfront Trail, the sound of voices and footsteps is awakening waterfront areas from Niagara to Trenton. Across Halton the Waterfront Trail is routed through parks and natural areas, one of the world's finest botanical gardens, and past busy marinas and quiet residential neighbourhoods. Trail users are rewarded with frequent views of the lake, along with insights into the history that shaped the waterfront communities of Oakville and Burlington. That history includes a long period of neglect for the needs of the waterfront and the more recent story of its regeneration.

People have long been attracted to the water's edge, originally because it provided easy transportation and abundant resources. The mouths of Bronte and Sixteen Mile Creeks provided natural harbours, and fleets of fishing boats once ventured onto Lake Ontario. But these early settlers had little understanding of humans'

Man and beast enjoying the Lake Ontario Waterfront Trail.
SCOTT ROBERTSON

role as part of nature and often exploited resources with little thought of the long-term consequences.

By the 1850s, 43,000 tons of rock per year were being removed from the shoreline to provide construction materials and ballast for ships. Stone-hooking, as it was called, removed loose rocks from beaches and shallow waters. These rocks are the lake's natural armour; removing them accelerated erosion along the shoreline and destroyed valuable fish habitats.

Other acts of negligence and ignorance also gradually changed the waters of Lake Ontario from pristine to polluted. The waterfront became a convenient dumping place for industrial effluents and sewage. Beaches were contaminated and fish became inedible. Many communities turned their backs on the waterfront as this once thriving nucleus of culture and commerce declined.

Finally, in the 1970s, public concerns about the neglected waterfront began to be heard. Municipalities and the provincial government responded with improved sewage treatment plants and regulations controlling the discharge of industrial wastes into the lake.

Meanwhile conservation authorities and municipalities began acquiring land along the waterfront. Since 1987 Halton Region Conservation Authority, the City of Burlington and Halton Region have been purchasing cottage lands and leases at Beachway Park for recreational use and to protect significant dune and beach habitats. One of the busiest sections of the Waterfront Trail now runs through this parkland which has been reclaimed for public use.

About the same time, the conservation authority began to develop a shoreline management program to address the flooding and erosion problems that damage both the shoreline ecosystem and lakefront property. The shoreline management program has six primary components: protection measures, prevention guidelines, an inventory of the natural environment, monitoring natural processes and water levels, emergency response during storms and high-water periods, and public information.

This kind of coordinated planning fits well with the broader perspective provided by the Royal Commission on the Future of the Toronto Waterfront, headed by David Crombie. It was recognized that waterfront issues cannot be addressed in isolation, but must be seen as part of an ecosystem in which everything is connected. Air, water, land and all living organisms, including humans, are related in a complex web of interactions. For example, many species of Lake Ontario fish migrate into streams or wetlands to reproduce. In an ecosystem, decisions made upstream will affect downstream fish populations.

With this in mind, the Royal Commission stressed the importance of the Greater Toronto Bioregion — bounded by the Niagara Escarpment on the west, Oak Ridges Moraine on the north, and Lake Ontario to the south — as an interconnected system. Natural geographic units, particularly watersheds, are the critical connecting elements within the system. Over fifty-six creeks and rivers drain into Lake Ontario from within the bioregion. In Halton alone, from Grindstone Creek in the west to Joshua's Creek in the east, seventeen watercourses enter the lake. An ecosystem approach to planning is essential to address the complex ecological, economic, and community issues that confront Lake Ontario communities.

Sunrise fishing on Lake Ontario, Bronte Harbour, Oakville.
SANDY BELL

The Waterfront Trail is a great way to reintroduce people to the waterfront; it is also a symbol of the waterfront's regeneration. The trail is a visible and identifiable link between communities along the waterfront. In Halton it loops along 36 kilometres of shoreline, much of which is in residential neighbourhoods. Along the way, the trail links together historic harbours that are being revitalized by recreational boating, beaches where sailboarders and sunseekers come to play, and natural woodlands where birds and butterflies gather on their annual migrations.

The Waterfront Trail in Halton is especially rich in human history, as the shoreline was one of the first areas of European settlement in Halton. This heritage is reflected in what remains of the grand lakeshore estates once owned by wealthy families, and in the more modest houses clustered around now historic fishing harbours.

Many of Halton's waterfront parks also reflect the watershed's cultural roots. The Brant Inn, demolished in 1969, graced the western edge of Spencer Smith Park in Burlington. In its heyday, the inn attracted musical greats such as Ella Fitzgerald, Benny Goodman and Lena Horne. Spencer Smith Park was named for a former president of the Burlington Horticultural Society.

McNichol Park, at the mouth of Shoreacres Creek, is also associated with prominent Canadians. The property was part of a tract of land granted to Laura Secord in 1809. Later it was sold to W. D. Flatt, a Burlington developer, and Cyrus A. Birge, a founding board member of the Canadian Screw Company. Birge's daughter, Edythe MacKay, built the lavish mansion Shoreacres in 1931. The property, later called McNichol Estates, was acquired by the City of Burlington in 1990.

Another site of historical interest is the Sovereign House and Mazo de la Roche Heritage Display Centre in Bronte Bluffs Park. The house, built in 1825, is one of the oldest surviving dwellings in Halton. It was

A TALL SHIP CONJURES UP IMAGES OF THE PAST AT BRONTE HARBOUR, OAKVILLE. MAGGIE MILLS

the home of Charles Sovereign, one of Bronte's founding fathers. Canadian writer Mazo de la Roche also lived here from 1911 to 1914 and based her novel *Possession* on her time in Bronte.

These sites and many others along the Waterfront Trail give a sense of how human uses of the waterfront have changed over time. Flora and fauna have also changed because of the loss of critical habitat. The same rocky lakebed that attracted stone-hookers to shallow offshore waters now provides ideal conditions for millions of zebra mussels, which were recently introduced to the Great Lakes from ships' ballast water. Migrating waterfowl have readily adapted to this new food source, and the Halton shoreline now hosts spectacular late-winter concentrations of diving ducks such as scaup, goldeneye and scoters.

The Waterfront Trail introduces visitors to many of the natural and cultural gems along the Burlington and Oakville shore. By putting people in touch with their waterfront, it helps build a sense of community stewardship. With the combined efforts of governments at all levels, industry and citizens, an ever-improving waterfront will be our legacy to the next generation.

Watershed Guidepost
Waterfront Trail, Oakville and Burlington

The 325-kilometre Waterfront Trail, connecting communities and green spaces from Niagara to Trenton, is part of the waterfront regeneration activities that are guided by nine principles — clean, open, diverse, green, accessible, affordable, connected, usable and attractive. The trail offers a variety of recreational experiences, such as walking, cycling, birding, and boating, and visiting cultural heritage sites. Parts of the trail are wheelchair accessible. The trail is marked by directional signs to help users follow its course. The Waterfront Trail Guidebook provides maps and detailed information on natural and cultural attractions along the trail.

Directions: The western end of Halton's Waterfront Trail can be reached either through the Royal Botanical Gardens or across the Burlington Canal into Beachway Park. The trail connects many parks and historical sites — LaSalle, Bronte Harbour, Fisherman's Wharf, Vista Promenade and Water's Edge park. East of Water's Edge is Coronation Park, the site of the annual Oakville Waterfront Festival. In the Oakville Harbour area, attractions include Tannery Park, Shipyard Park, Navy Flats and Busby Park, Civic Park, Erchless Estate and Lakeside Park. The Waterfront Trail leaves Halton at Arkendo Park, where Joshua's Creek empties into Lake Ontario.

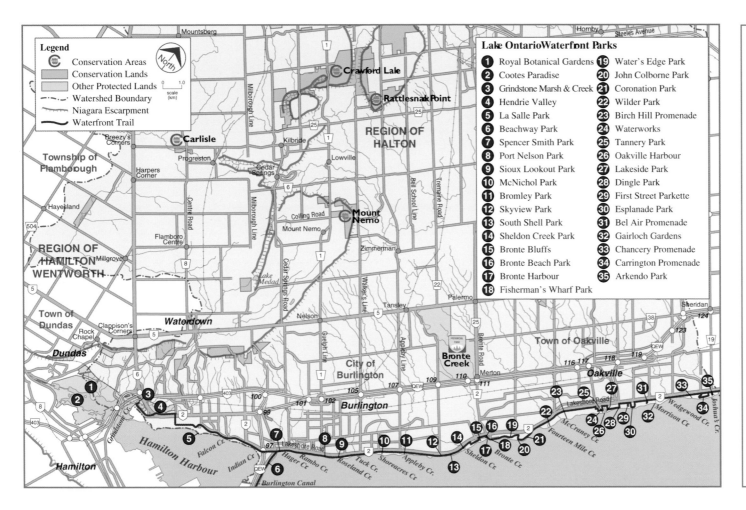

Lake Ontario Waterfront Parks

1. Royal Botanical Gardens
2. Cootes Paradise
3. Grindstone Marsh & Creek
4. Hendrie Valley
5. La Salle Park
6. Beachway Park
7. Spencer Smith Park
8. Port Nelson Park
9. Sioux Lookout Park
10. McNichol Park
11. Bromley Park
12. Skyview Park
13. South Shell Park
14. Sheldon Creek Park
15. Bronte Bluffs
16. Bronte Beach Park
17. Bronte Harbour
18. Fisherman's Wharf Park
19. Water's Edge Park
20. John Colborne Park
21. Coronation Park
22. Wilder Park
23. Birch Hill Promenade
24. Waterworks
25. Tannery Park
26. Oakville Harbour
27. Lakeside Park
28. Dingle Park
29. First Street Parkette
30. Esplanade Park
31. Bel Air Promenade
32. Gairloch Gardens
33. Chancery Promenade
34. Carrington Promenade
35. Arkendo Park

Nature Calls – Island of Green and Caspian Terns

The Waterfront Trail is always a great place to view waterbirds, especially during spring and fall migration. One natural haunt worth a visit is the trail and lookout on the northeastern shore of Burlington Bay, just north of the Canada Centre for Inland Waters. Three new islands have been built to create habitat for colonies of nesting birds. The area is now home to one of the largest populations of common and Caspian terns in the lower Great Lakes. Be sure to wear a hat when viewing this natural spectacle of up to a thousand black-and-white birds with brilliant orange beaks. Listen for the low-pitched *kaah, kaah* of the Caspian tern as it circles above and dives headfirst into the bay in search of fish.

ROBERT McCAW

Enjoying a Sunday afternoon stroll on Bronte pier, Oakville. Mark Zelinski

FISHING ON OAKVILLE PIER IN A BRILLIANT MORNING SKY. MAGGIE MILLS

MISTY MORRISON CREEK GENTLY FLOWS INTO LAKE ONTARIO AT GAIRLOCH GARDENS, OAKVILLE. SCOTT ROBERTSON

PHOTOGRAPHER ROSEMARIE KEOUGH CAPTURES THE BEAUTY OF ROADSIDE FLOWERS DURING AUTUMN. PAT KEOUGH

14

ARTISANS OF THE NATURAL LANDSCAPE

Among my fondest memories as a boy growing up in Bruce County, Ontario, were the ramblings over the family farm. The land was carved in half by Deer Creek and I was forever exploring its banks. Herons, dragonflies, kingfishers and muskrats provided hours of fascination, but the kingfisher was always my favourite. Hearing their rattling calls and watching their spectacular dives for fish stirred feelings inside me that perhaps only a naturalist truly understands. When I moved to Halton County, my need to explore did not diminish and local conservation lands became my new Deer Creek. Within a short walk or drive I could be at the Mountsberg Conservation Area, the Shanahan Forest Tract or Hilton Falls. In the late 1970s, these places became even more important as I began to seriously pursue nature photography. Since that time, my search for pictures has taken me to almost all of the protected lands in the Halton watershed. To me, the significance of these wild places reaches far beyond photography. On an early morning last May, I sat on an uprooted tree in a watery swamp somewhere in the Shanahan Forest Tract. From across the tangle of downed trees and rotting stumps came the ringing song of a northern waterthrush. Those boyhood feelings came rushing back. May these lands endure.

ROBERT McCAW, WILDLIFE PHOTOGRAPHER

The Halton watershed is awash in nature's sensual patterns and textures. From the grand panoramic views of Mount Nemo and Rattlesnake Point to the simple beauty of wildflowers, rocks, and creeks, artists and photographers are inspired by the region's diversity and splendour. Whether growing up in the watershed or adopting it as home, artists have an intimate relationship with the land; they frequently visit favourite haunts, capturing the subtle changes of the seasons and portraying nature's rhythms and moods.

"Throughout the seasons this unique landscape provides me with a neverending source of images to paint. I love to paint that special look winter brings, wrapping the landscape in a blanket of snow. Even in a Canadian winter there is a sense of security and protection throughout the valleys. Textures like moss-covered limestone, weathered, old barns and rusty machinery are abundant. Halton's many creeks that flow through the countryside create scenic waterfalls and provide food and shelter for wildlife along the

Antique stained-glass windows sparkle in the morning sun, Campbellville. GARY HUTTON

way. I hope we appreciate what is in our own backyard and through conservation can continue to enjoy its unique beauty," writes Brian Darcy, a Waterdown artist.

In the conservation lands, artists find infinite images in the unspoiled wilderness and countryside. Robert Bateman, artist and naturalist, has explored Canada's wild frontiers but he is also deeply attached to the local landscapes of the Halton watershed. Brian Darcy, who emigrated to Canada with his family at age seven, also has a special connection with the countryside around the Niagara Escarpment. Robert McCaw, a wildlife photographer, displays an intimate vision of nature as he captures the subtle beauty and textures of wildlife.

Robert Ross was raised in the Burlington and Hamilton area. Naturally he gravitated to the conservation lands in the watershed. In his paintings, Ross looks at these places and various elements of the landscape as symbols. Places such as Cootes Paradise — only miles away from

Hamilton's steel mills and city streets — are sanctuaries that balance urban life with a connection to nature. Ross's art heightens our awareness of the need for environmental protection. The Burlington Fine Arts Association has a nucleus of six to ten people who paint outdoors every week in a different location. They call themselves the *Plein Air* painters after the French Impressionists. Light, colour, landforms, nature's rhythms and moods — all inspire these artists. Lois Crawford, a member of the group, says that the landscape gives them energy. This close connection with the land has fostered an environmental awareness and strong conservation ethic among these artists.

Artisans and antique dealers have also gravitated to the Halton watershed, converting nineteenth-century homes and barns into galleries and studios. A ramble along the backroads of "Escarpment Country" — the historic township of Nassagaweya and the hamlets of Brookville, Moffat and Campbellville — unearths valuable heirlooms from Ontario's rural past. Campbellville, the largest of the three hamlets, preserves its appeal as an early twentieth-century crossroads community. A walk down the main street overwhelms visitors with the eclectic collection of antiques, nostalgia and curiosities. Chris Burnett, a Campbellville artist, captures the essence of this village and rural Halton county in her charismatic and nostalgic "Heritage Paintings," portraying the sights and sounds of today against a backdrop of local history.

In Campbellville visitors can find just about everything from stained glass, pottery, pine furniture and original paintings to home-baked goods. Margaret Lott renovated her 1891 home and opened the *Lott's and Lots* bakery, specializing in cakes, pies and cookies. The *Stone House of Campbellville*, one of the oldest-operating antique shops in the area is located

Culinary artisan Margaret Lott, holds fresh apple pies near a hand-carved sign made by Dakota Mill signmaker of Lowville, Campbellville. GARY HUTTON

on Guelph Line outside the village of Campbellville,. It is a beguiling place with antique stained-glass windows displayed outside. The windows, constructed using the old cane-lead technique, have been recovered from old homes, buildings and churches in England and Scotland.

In the village of Moffat, 10 kilometres northwest of Campbellville, is *Old Is Beautiful Antiques*, which has a wonderful selection of early pine furniture, primitives, and country accents. The antique shop is set in a unique mid-nineteenth-century barn. Another shop not to miss is the *Loghouse Gallery*. Nestled in a beautiful woodland setting near the Yaremko-Ridley Resource Management Area, the gallery is an oasis away from the din of city life. The gallery, which has operated for twenty years, features handmade stoneware, pottery, wood turnings, wrought iron and jewellery by Ontario artisans. It is worth the trip down country roads to browse through these shops.

The urban centres of Burlington, Oakville and Milton have active public arts programs. For twenty years, the Burlington Arts Centre has been the foundation for visual arts in the community. It is the seventh-largest public art gallery in Ontario. The centre offers courses in drawing and painting, rug hooking, woodcarving, photography, quilting and pottery. Oakville Galleries is a public art gallery committed to contemporary Canadian art. There are two locations: the Centennial Gallery at Oakville Public Library, and Gairloch Gallery located at Gairloch Gardens. Milton boasts two art associations: Arts Milton, an umbrella group for the performing, literary and visual arts; and the Fine Art Society of Milton which hosts an annual art festival. It's apparent from the diversity of these creative voices that a vibrant artistic community thrives in the cities and countryside of the Halton watershed.

Eden Mill's illustrator Janet Wilson captures the sugar bush on canvas for a children's storybook, Campbellville. Gary Hutton

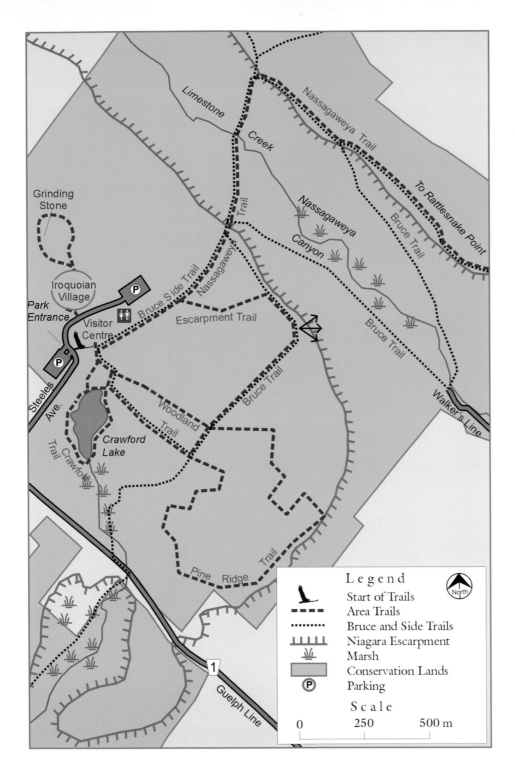

Watershed Guidepost
Crawford Lake Conservation Area, Milton

Nature brings out the artist in everyone. For a brief moment, we would like to capture the perfection of a sunrise or fall colours reflecting in a still, aquamarine lake. Crawford Lake Conservation Area is particularly enticing to amateur and professional artists and photographers, as it overflows with nature's resplendent charm.

A rare meromictic lake that holds clues to the cultural and natural history of the Halton area is the centrepiece of the conservation area. The one-kilometre boardwalk around the lake has interpretive plaques on the lake's natural history. Surrounding the lake is a unique woodland ecosystem that supports delicate plants, such as maidenhair spleenwort ferns, roundleaf sundew, and rare orchids, such as yellow lady's slipper.

Venture beyond the lake and explore the extensive woodlands, open meadows, pine plantations and escarpment features. The woodland trail leads to a spectacular lookout over the Nassagaweya Canyon. For a longer hike, the Nassagaweya Trail crosses the canyon and follows the cliff edge to Rattlesnake Point.

Families can enjoy the quiet pleasure of a walk in the woods and witness the changing colours of nature throughout the year, from spring wildflowers to fall leaves. The hiker's code "Take only pictures, leave only footprints" should always be respected, so bring your camera or sketchbook and learn to observe nature with fresh eyes.

Directions: From Highway 401, take Guelph Line south (Exit 312) to Steeles Avenue, then turn east to the park entrance. From the QEW, take Guelph Line north (Exit 102) to Steeles Avenue, then turn east to the park entrance.

Nature Calls - Wildflowers and Cedar Waxwings

There's nothing more fleeting or beautiful than woodland wildflowers in early spring. At Crawford Lake, you can witness a rainbow of ephemerals such as white trillium, trout lily, May apple, wake robin and spring beauty. Sit quietly and you can even hear the gentle crackles of flattened winter leaves being lifted by emerald green shoots pushing skyward. When the wildflowers peak around the middle of May, watch for the arrival of one of nature's most artistically tailored birds. The cedar waxwing's finely sculptured brown feathers are brightened by a dash of red and yellow. Listen for its lispy *zee zee* song, announcing the grand finale of the wildflower spectacle.

ROBERT McCAW

Visitors enjoy an early spring view of Nassagaweya Canyon at Crawford Lake Conservation Area, Milton. Sandy Bell

Inset: Hepatica are among the first wildflowers to appear in spring. Neil Hester

YOUNG EASTERN COTTONTAIL RABBITS NEST ON THE NIAGARA ESCARPMENT. ROBERT McCAW

Inset: SCARLET CUP MUSHROOMS BRIGHTEN THE FOREST FLOOR IN EARLY SPRING. RICHARD ARMSTRONG

Wildlife photographer Robert McCaw patiently waits for wild subjects to appear, Moffat.   Robert McCaw

Inset: folk artist Chris Burnett works on a new painting of Arawana Farm at night
with the escarpment and Glen Eden ski area in the background, Campbellville.   Gary Fliss

STUDENTS EXPLORE ANCIENT CEDARS AND LIMESTONE CLIFFS OF THE NIAGARA ESCARPMENT, KELSO CONSERVATION AREA, MILTON. MARK ZELINSKI

15

LANDS FOR LEARNING AND RAPTOR RAPTURE

Arriving in Burlington at the age of eight, I believe my love of the countryside was already instilled in me, as I had been exposed to the lush Yorkshire dales of England. My path to Halton's conservation lands was through involvement with an active Scout troop in Burlington. Within fifteen minutes, we drove from city to countryside, anticipating another challenging adventure and a new area to explore. From the dank, cool caves at Mount Nemo, to the cliffs of Rattlesnake Point and the many creeks and waterfalls of Halton, we hiked though an environment that was rich in wildlife and diverse in terrain. Winter camping at Camp Manitou, rafting down Bronte Creek, planting trees — all gave me a strong connection to the land. This connection led me to pursue a career as a painter. For over twenty-five years, I have focused my work on the portrayal of farms, people and animals that co-exist with the landscape. My paintings also try to convey an appreciation and understanding of the natural environment. Halton's countryside is truly inspirational as well as being a great place for learning and outdoor education.

BRIAN DARCY, LANDSCAPE PAINTER, WATERDOWN

Environmental education can transform our perception of the natural world, break down our misconceptions about nature and inspire a new conservation ethic. Activities that allow children and adults to experience direct contact with nature create a lasting impression. Often these experiences begin in childhood with a first awakening to the mysteries of nature and develop, in adulthood, into a lasting commitment to the environment.

Environmental education is really the study of nature. Learning about nature through accurate observation enables us to thread beads of information together into a harmonious whole and leads us to understanding and appreciation. Environmental education also gives people practical and helpful knowledge about the natural world, of which humans are a part.

Nature study cultivates a child's imagination in much the same way as fairy tales and nursery rhymes. There are so many wonderful and true stories that can be read from nature. These natural-history stories

Waterdown artist, Brian Darcy, paints an image of a great horned owl at Mount Nemo, with a live bird from the Mountsberg Wildlife Centre as his subject, Campbellville.
GARY FLISS

help children express things as they are and instill a love of nature that can last a lifetime. In the *Handbook of Nature Study*, written in 1911, Anna Comstock eloquently states that "Nature study cultivates in the child a love of the beautiful; it brings to him early a perception of colour, form and music. He sees whatever there is in his environment, whether it be the thunderhead piled up in the western sky, or the golden flash of the oriole in the elm; whether it be the purple of the shadows on the snow, or the azure glint on the wing of the little butterfly. Also, what there is of sound, he hears; he reads the music score of the bird orchestra, separating each part and knowing which bird sings it. And the patter of the rain, the gurgle of the brook, the sighing of the wind in the pine, he notes and loves and becomes enriched thereby." This still holds true, perhaps even more so today.

The Halton watershed has an abundance of environmental education opportunities for children and families. The Royal Botanical Gardens, Bronte

Creek Provincial Park, museums and cultural centres, and the Halton Region Conservation Authority all have well-developed outdoor education programs. For years the Crawford Lake and Mountsberg Conservation Areas have been providing excellent natural and cultural history programs to thousands of students and teachers. These programs also provide opportunities for the public to experience the principles necessary to sustain the natural environment of the watershed — understanding, appreciation and protection.

The Crawford Lake Conservation Area's unique blend of natural and cultural treasures provided the perfect ingredients for the conservation learning centre that has been established at the area. The conservation area has a year-round education program that includes guided walks, demonstrations and special events. Programs for students and organized groups include activities such as simulated archaeological digs and experiences in the reconstructed Iroquoian Village, where children gain a sense of a lifestyle that has long passed. Four major themes — archaeology, Native heritage, conservation and the Niagara Escarpment — demonstrate the importance of this area in Ontario's prehistory and natural history. Programs such as "Sweet Water Season," "Season of the Three Sisters," and "Autumn on the Escarpment" celebrate the rich natural environment of Halton and how its early people lived in harmony with nature.

The Mountsberg Conservation Area is a 446-hectare park located in the towns of Milton and Flamborough and the township of Puslinch. The

Children discover wetland critters from a pond boardwalk at the Mountsberg Conservation Area, Campbellville.
Conservation Halton

area includes a 202-hectare water-control lake, significant wetlands and a large forest ecosystem. The area is also an important wildlife sanctuary and education centre outfitted with 14 kilometres of trails, a demonstration farm and sugar bush, and a year-round education program. The area also includes the Douglas G. Cockburn Raptor Centre. As a result of collisions with wires and vehicles, and other human-made hazards, raptors — hawks, vultures, owls and eagles — can be seriously injured and require special attention. The raptor centre includes an avian hospital with receiving, treatment and recovery areas. Eighty percent of the birds treated at the raptor centre are returned to the wild. Birds with permanent disabilities remain at Mountsberg in special enclosures as part of the conservation education program. Healthy raptors are also relocated from Pearson International Airport because of the potential hazard they create there and are released at Mountsberg. The large expanse of natural habitat and its close proximity to the Niagara Escarpment and Lake Ontario make Mountsberg a perfect location for the release program. The Raptor Centre also includes an exhibit gallery, a theatre and outdoor flyway for presentations with live birds of prey. This combination of wildlife rehabilitation and environmental education is unique in Ontario.

Mountsberg is also the location of a bird-banding program operated by a dedicated group of volunteers. Numbered metal rings placed on the legs of birds provide important information for the study of migration routes, breeding habitats, age and flight patterns. Since 1976 more than one hundred thousand birds have been banded at Mountsberg. This data is helping scientists learn more about birds, information that ultimately will help to protect them.

Acquainting children with the patterns of nature through interpretive programs will help to create a better environment in the future. Many children's range of experience is limited to urban centres. Summer camp allows children to immerse themselves in nature. The Mountsberg Wildlife Centre is the base camp for the "Ways of the Woods" program. The day camp, available to children eight to twelve years of age, operates during July and August. Campers visit Kelso, Mount Nemo and Crawford Lake Conservation Areas. Environmental activities such as pond explorations, insect hunts and bird hikes encourage a better understanding of the watershed's natural resources. At Crawford Lake Conservation Area, children participate in a simulated archaeological dig, through which they gain an appreciation of our cultural heritage. These experiences from childhood — summer camp, a walk in the woods, a canoe trip — remain in our memories and affect our relationship with nature.

Through our contact with nature and environmental education, we may nurture a conservation ethic that emphasizes an appreciation and an understanding of the natural world and our place within the ecosystem.

STUDENTS PLAY A NATIVE GAME WHILE TOURING THE IROQUOIAN VILLAGE AT CRAWFORD LAKE CONSERVATION AREA. SANDY BELL

With knowledge comes the wisdom to make informed choices. As we recognize that we are all interrelated parts of the ecosystem, we begin to make decisions that are sustainable not only for this generation but future generations. The conservation lands of the Halton watershed are truly excellent lands for learning.

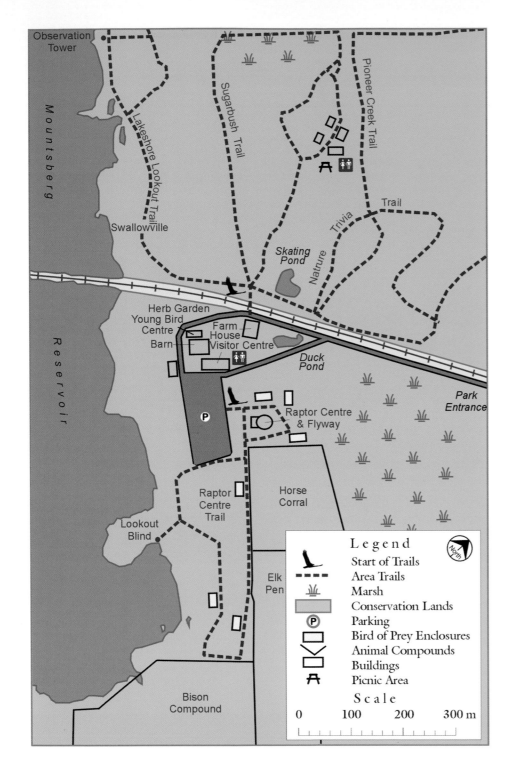

Legend

(bird)	Start of Trails
- - -	Area Trails
(marsh)	Marsh
(box)	Conservation Lands
P	Parking
▽	Bird of Prey Enclosures
☐	Animal Compounds
☐	Buildings
⚘	Picnic Area

Scale

0   100   200   300 m

Watershed Guidepost
Raptor Centre, Mountsberg Conservation Area, Campbellville

Gazing into the large yellow eyes of a great horned owl awakens a powerful human response. Birds of prey are amazing to watch in the wild, but the opportunity to observe hawks and owls up close is indeed rare and exhilarating. This experience is available at the Mountsberg Conservation Area while walking along the Douglas G. Cockburn Raptor Centre Trail. This 1.6-kilometre trail features nonreleasable birds of prey in special enclosures that allow visitors to view the birds at close range. The Raptor Centre, located at the start of the trail, has an exhibit gallery on birds of prey that includes hundreds of photographs and mounted specimens.

Year-round programs at Mountsberg encourage people to experience and learn about nature. On frosty winter evenings, naturalists conduct exciting Owl Prowls through snow-laden pine woods. During these hikes, visitors, using their newly acquired hooting skills, listen and watch for the elusive creatures to appear. Staff naturalists also lead night hikes to observe bats in their natural surroundings. In this program, visitors learn about the importance of bats to the ecosystem and about echolocation, an incredible adaptation that bats have developed for nocturnal hunting. A visit to Mountsberg Wildlife Centre gives new insight into birds of prey and other fascinating creatures with which we share our bioregion.

Directions: From Highway 401, take Guelph Line south (Exit 312) to Reid Side Road, west to Second Side Road, south to Campbellville Road, west to Milborough Line, then turn north to park entrance. From the QEW, take Guelph Line north (Exit 102) to Campbellville Road, turn west to Milborough Line, then turn north to the park entrance.

Nature Calls - Osprey Angling

Near the end of the Raptor Centre Trail, along the shore of Mountsberg Lake, keep your eyes open and ears sharp for nature's only fish hawk. Hovering above the lake's quiet waters, the osprey watches for signs of its prey just below the surface. Dropping rapidly with feet extended and wings folded back, the bird strikes the water with a thunderous splash. Sharp, curved talons with spike-like projections help the black-and-white hawk hold on to slippery fish. Listen for the osprey's short, sharp *chewk, chewk* whistle as the bird lands on a nearby nesting platform specifically built for these incredible birds of prey.

ROBERT McCAW

STUDENTS MAKE EYE CONTACT WITH LIVE BIRDS OF PREY IN DOUGLAS COCKBURN RAPTOR CENTRE AT MOUNTSBERG CONSERVATION AREA, CAMPBELLVILLE. SANDY BELL

Inset: THE RAPTOR CENTRE EXHIBIT GALLERY ON BIRDS OF PREY. CONSERVATION HALTON

ORNITHOLOGIST DAVE BREWER REMOVES SMALL BIRDS CAUGHT IN A MIST NET, MOUNTSBERG CONSERVATION AREA, CAMPBELLVILLE. ROBERT McCAW

Inset: METAL BANDS ARE PLACED ON THE BIRDS' LEGS TO LEARN MORE ABOUT THEIR HABITS. ROBERT McCAW

CHILDREN LOOK THROUGH A ONE-WAY VIEWING WINDOW INTO THE RAPTOR HOSPITAL FROM THE AERIE THEATRE, WHICH IS OUTFITTED WITH A PEREGRINE FALCON EXHIBIT, MOUNTSBERG CONSERVATION AREA, CAMPBELLVILLE. GARY FLISS

FARMLAND SURROUNDS THE PROTECTED CONSERVATION LANDS OF RATTLESNAKE POINT CONSERVATION AREA, MILTON. SANDY BELL

16

RISING, WILD AND PROTECTED — Conservation Halton

As a boy I grew up in Tansley, on a small family farm in the north end of Burlington. On Saturdays, especially during the fall, I would head out on lengthy bicycle jaunts. My favourite route was along Dundas Highway (there was hardly any traffic in the fifties) and north up Walkers Line to 10 Side Road, or what is today Derry Road, and complete my loop by heading down Appleby Line. It was on these magical journeys that I encountered four significant things: the limestone majesty of the Niagara Escarpment, the breathtaking scale of Mount Nemo, the almost touchable proximity of Rattlesnake Point and a dream that somehow, someday, I would actually live on the escarpment, as close to the scarp face as possible. Well, the dream came true. Five hectares just east of Rattlesnake Point has been the Penman family home for what will soon be thirty years. Each of those years has been a privilege — each day, each season and each year. But my favourite moments are when I look out over a fifty-kilometre vista at daybreak and watch the sun rise and the landscape below slowly emerge out of the frequently heavy morning fog. Very early on, I realized that the sustainability of the escarpment and of our watershed was of critical importance, and with this recognition I became a director of the Halton Region Conservation Authority — almost twenty years ago. I am particularly proud of the accomplishments of this organization. Land acquisitions, careful management of natural resources, environmental education programs, and an ongoing concern for people, property and the well-being of our citizens has created a legacy with roots firmly planted for the benefit of future generations.

BRIAN PENMAN, CHAIR, HALTON REGION CONSERVATION AUTHORITY

The health of our society is connected to our watersheds. It is not an idle metaphor to say that rivers are our lifeblood. Rivers have shaped our geological and cultural history. From the time of our aboriginal people and the pioneers, we have depended on our rivers for survival, whether as transportation routes, as natural resources and waterpower, or simply for the water we drink. In the future, we will continue to depend on our rivers, and the vitality of our watersheds will affect the sustainability of our society. For over fifty years, Ontario's conservation authorities have recognized the importance of our watersheds and have been committed to protecting the natural resources within them.

Ontario's watersheds, however, have not always been protected. In the pursuit of economic progress, our natural resources were long exploited

Protecting Halton's creeks creates a healthy watershed environment, Bronte Creek, Oakville.
CONSERVATION HALTON

— wetlands were drained, forests cleared and streams diverted. By the 1930s, water quality had drastically deteriorated. Rivers had become "open sewers" flowing with industrial and municipal waste. Deforestation had accentuated the cycle of spring floods and summer droughts. Wildlife habitat was in jeopardy.

A nascent conservation movement developed as a reaction to this environmental degradation. Concerned citizens, amateur naturalists and academics formed its foundation with the restoration and conservation of natural resources as their unified objective. In the 1930s, the municipalities of the Grand River area attempted to deal with issues of flooding, pollution and low summer flows. In response to the severe floods of 1929, the Grand River Valley Board of Trade was formed. It urged a regionwide approach to the problems and financial support from the province. By 1938 eight municipalities had formed the Grand River Conservation Commission, which became a prototype for conservation authorities.

In 1941 the Guelph Conference was held to discuss the possibility of providing meaningful and productive work for returning war veterans as workers in conservation programs. The conference called for the restoration and protection of all natural resources within Southern Ontario. The seminal idea to emerge from the conference was that conservation planning must be based on a watershed approach that considers all natural resources as inseparable parts in an interconnected system.

Following the Guelph Conference, the Federal Advisory Committee on Reconstruction sponsored a survey in the Ganaraska watershed. A. H. Richardson, a government forest engineer and later the first director of the province's Conservation Board, wrote the survey. *The Ganaraska Report* espoused a holistic approach to natural resource management or, as it is now known, "watershed planning." This progressive principle of linking land and water management is the hallmark of the conservation authority philosophy. Conservation authorities are considered pioneers in watershed and ecosystem planning.

The Conservation Authorities Act, established in 1946, was the culmination of the combined effort of these conservation-oriented groups. Two authorities, Ausauble River and Etobicoke River, were formed in the first year. In the wake of Hurricane Hazel's destruction in 1954, municipalities and the province renewed their support for the formation of

A water-control reservoir helps prevent floods and augment low creek flows, Kelso Conservation Area, Milton.
SANDY BELL

conservation authorities. Halton Region Conservation Authority was established in 1963 with the amalgamation of Sixteen Mile Creek (formed in 1956) and Twelve Mile Creek (formed in 1958) Conservation Authorities, and the enlargement of those watersheds to include the drainage basins of Grindstone and Joshua's Creeks.

Today there are thirty-eight conservation authorities across Ontario. They are community-based environmental-protection agencies that work in partnership with the provincial government, munici-palities, and regional governments. Three principles embody the concept of conservation authorities: local initiative, cost-sharing, and watershed jurisdiction. Citizens in a watershed must ask the Ontario government to form an authority, and local people are appointed to the corporate body. The cost of projects is shared by the municipalities within the watershed, along with funds from the provincial government for specific programs. Management decisions are based on natural boundaries such as river valleys, rather than arbitrary political boundaries such as county lines. Each conservation authority manages the natural resources in its watershed to reflect the needs of the local community and the health of rivers and creeks.

In the last fifty years, conservation authorities have made significant strides in remedying over a century of environmental degradation. Water quality is a primary concern. Conservation authorities work closely with landowners and various levels of government to improve the quality of water flowing into rivers and streams. Flooding has virtually been eliminated due to structures such as dams and dikes that protect communities, while regulation of development on floodplains and wetlands prevents future floods. In the Halton watershed, four water-control structures were built to provide flood protection, prevent erosion, improve stream flows and create recreational opportunities. Over 2,000 kilometres of flood plain and fill-line mapping has also been produced to protect natural waterways.

Environmental planning is another important conservation authority program that includes watercourse regulations, watershed studies, natural heritage stewardship, ecosystem restoration and managing forests — each concerned with the health of our watershed.

We have rediscovered our creeks and natural areas as a sanctuary from urban life. The Halton Region Conservation Authority was the first organization in Halton to create conservation lands on the Niagara Escarpment. The conservation authority has also protected significant areas of Carolinian forest, wetlands and wildlife habitat. Regional and local municipalities, the provincial government and the Royal Botanical Gardens have also acquired conservation lands in the Halton watershed. More than 5,500 hectares of significant lands are now protected. Each year thousands of visitors enjoy the conservation lands of the Halton watershed.

Into the next century, we will continue to need conservation authorities to protect our watersheds. The lands and creeks of the Halton watershed are constantly under threat from development and encroaching urbanization. Knowledge of the unique features of the watershed can help foster an appreciation of the natural world and a responsibility to preserve the ecosystem. If Halton's natural spaces are to remain wild, we must all work together to protect them.

Inset: Founding member of Sixteen Mile Creek Conservation Authority, Allan Day, at Hilton Falls reflecting on the authority's wise decision to acquire the falls in 1963. Diane Leblovic

A painting of Hilton Falls by artist Paul Duff, was given to Allan Day from his family on his 75th birthday. Conservation Halton

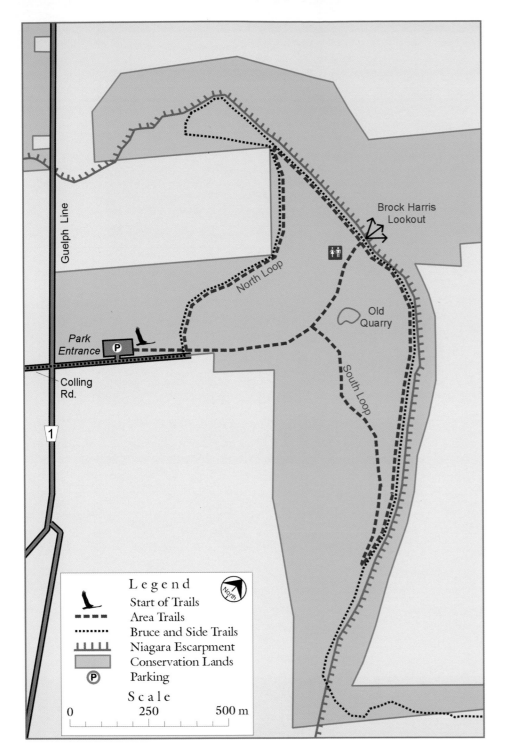

Legend

↟ Start of Trails

– – – Area Trails

········· Bruce and Side Trails

⊥⊥⊥⊥ Niagara Escarpment

▭ Conservation Lands

Ⓟ Parking

Scale

0   250   500 m

Watershed Guidepost
Mount Nemo Conservation Area, Burlington

On a crisp autumn day, Mount Nemo Conservation Area is a great place for a hike. Brock Harris Lookout, 295 metres above sea level, has a spectacular vista from which to view the trees changing colours and 50 kilometres of countryside. From this height you can also watch migrating birds of prey circling below in the valley. There is a singular pleasure in watching this flight of freedom from such a lofty perch.

The trails at Mount Nemo follow the cliff edge of the Niagara Escarpment past a former quarry site and through open meadows. This natural environment park includes unique geological features and an excellent example of a cliff-edge ecosystem. As you walk along the trails, look at the eastern white cedars at the cliff edge. These diminutive gnarled trees are part of Ontario's oldest-growth forest. At the Brock Harris Lookout, there are interpretive plaques with information and illustrations on the natural history of the area.

The Mount Nemo Conservation Area, with crevice caves and ancient cedars, is a calming refuge from busy urban life.

Directions: From Highway 401, take Guelph Line south (Exit 312), then turn east at Colling Road to park entrance. From the QEW, take Guelph Line north (Exit 102), then turn east at Colling Road to park entrance.

Nature Calls - Wily Red Fox in a Quarry

As you walk the trails and take in the spectacular views from atop Mount Nemo, look for the wily red fox who resides in this area. The face of the red fox plainly shows how this mammal has been able to cope with human disturbances and still thrive. If ever a face showed cunning and extreme cleverness, it's that of the russet-red fox. You may only catch a glimpse of this fast runner, and more often only its bushy red tail with the white tip. The fox dens up in the crags of the old Mount Nemo quarry, which is slowly reclaiming its original nature. Listen too for the *yips* and *yelps* and coyote-like *barks* of the young pups in early summer.

ROBERT McCAW

The protection of Niagara Escarpment lands in the Halton watershed began with the acquisition of the Mount Nemo Conservation Area, Burlington. Sandy Bell

A RED-WINGED BLACKBIRD AT DAWN IN THE PROTECTED WETLAND OF THE MOUNTSBERG CONSERVATION AREA, TOWN OF FLAMBOROUGH. ROBERT McCAW

Left: A DRAGONFLY ON THIS BLUEFLAG SHOWS THE RICHNESS OF THE WETLANDS. ROBERT McCAW

Right: A YOUNG PILEATED WOODPECKER TAKES ITS FIRST LOOK AT THE OUTSIDE WORLD THROUGH NEST HOLE. ROBERT McCAW

THE CONSERVATION LANDS OF HALTON PROVIDE MANY RECREATIONAL AND EDUCATIONAL OPPORTUNITIES
FOR WATERSHED RESIDENTS AND VISITORS, KELSO CONSERVATION AREA, MILTON. NEIL HESTER

CONCLUSION

Clinging to the very edge of the precipitous cliff face of the Niagara Escarpment, amid a profusion of polypody fern in the Kelso Conservation Area, the gnarled white cedar didn't look very old. The trunk was less than 30 centimetres in diameter and the tree was certainly not very tall. How looks can be deceiving. The excitement in Professor Doug Larson's voice was infectious as he answered his own question: "This tree was already over two centuries old when Christopher Columbus sailed to North America, and here it is today, still living; in fact, thriving."

We remember well that spring day in 1989 spent rambling and scrambling along Halton's cliffs with Doug Larson. He and his colleagues from the University of Guelph had just made the remarkable discovery that eastern North America's oldest trees were located in the Kelso Conservation Area. In the months and years to follow, he found cedars of similar age, and even much older, living along the entire Niagara Escarpment from Niagara Falls to Tobermory. Together they represent one of the continent's most extensive old-growth forests.

There we were, with Doug, on the edge of scientific discovery, literally at the edge of the gleaming white cliff and at the edge of wilderness.

The ancient white cedar trees of Ontario's oldest growth forest were discovered on the Niagara Escarpment in Halton.
NEIL HESTER

Behind our backs was a maple-beech forest, leaves not yet unfurled, with wild ginger and white trilliums carpeting the earth. Below us, just beyond Kelso Lake, thousands of people whizzed by in automobiles along Highway 401, oblivious to the marvellous moment we were experiencing.

The Halton watershed, with its many conservation areas, charming backroads, farms and heritage homes, is an oasis of natural beauty and picturesque touches of mankind completely surrounded by encroaching urbanization. Situated midway between Hamilton and Toronto and traversed by two of Canada's busiest highways, the area provides an important refuge for a diverse range of plant and animal species — from rare orchids to salamanders, flying squirrels to turkey vultures, and from walking ferns to white-tailed deer. For humans caught up in an increasingly frenetic world, the Halton watershed is a refuge in another sense. Indeed, hundreds of thousands of people enjoy this region each year, partaking in a wide variety of educational and recreational activities.

Throughout the seasons, the Halton Region Conservation Authority presents a well-developed interpretive program to assist student and public visitors in learning about and appreciating the special nature of the watershed — the ancient cedars, the Niagara Escarpment, the meromictic Crawford Lake, and the Iroquoian village life and lore. At the Mountsberg Raptor Centre, the rehabilitation of injured owls and hawks is featured. And for sheer fun, whether it be sailboarding, boating, swimming, hiking, birdwatching, rock-climbing, mountain biking, picnicking, downhill and cross-country skiing, skating, sleigh riding or tobogganing, a myriad of recreational activities are to be enjoyed in the conservation lands.

The wonder is that all of this exists right on the doorstep of the most densely populated part of Canada. It was great foresight to have set aside and protected these marvellous lands in the Halton watershed. The challenge and the obligation will be to maintain the uncompromised integrity of these same lands, this natural legacy, as the future unfolds.

What an uplifting thought: if left undisturbed, the 700-year-old tree that so awed us that spring day will continue its slow growth through time. And one far-off day, perhaps centuries from now, other Halton hikers will thrill at its antiquity.

Pat Keough   Rosemarie Keough

Pat and Rosemarie Keough,

photographers, writers, and authors of The Niagara Escarpment: A Portfolio

ENJOYING WINTER ON CROSS-COUNTRY SKIS AT THE HILTON FALLS CONSERVATION AREA, MILTON. ROB STIMPSON

AFTERWORD

Halton: Rising, Wild and Beckoning is a celebration of the significant natural and cultural resources of the Halton watershed. And to astute readers, it is a recipe for a healthy lifestyle in touch with nature. The Watershed Guideposts include directions and ideas on how to explore the parks and conservation areas of the watershed. By communing with nature you will create lasting family memories and experience greater personal fulfillment.

The best way to enjoy this book is to respond to nature's beckoning call. Ecopsychologists suggest that communion with nature restores balance and harmony to our lives. "The nature of living beings is essentially wild," says Chellis Glendinning, a pioneer in the field of ecopsychology, and humans are no exception, having "evolved over millions of years through savannah, jungle and woodland to live in communion with the land. We exist instead dislocated from our roots by the psychological, philosophical and technological construction of our civilization . . ."

In simpler terms, nature is possibly the best antidote for the stress that is epidemic in our highly technological society. Ecopsychologists propose that it is possible to re-establish a connection with nature without returning to a primitive existence on the land. Reacquainting ourselves with nature can be achieved in hundreds of ways, especially in the conservation lands of the Halton watershed, where the opportunities seem endless.

The following checklist includes sixty-seven ways to connect with and to enjoy nature as part of everyday life. It has been prepared as a checklist so you can tick off the things you have done or want to do. The more activities you check off, the more you will find that your level of well-being and happiness increases. But take heed, the desire to engage in some of these things will be challenging as the demands of our technological society and daily tasks pull us back. Be daring, get to know the land, water and creatures with which we share this bioregion. As you explore the watershed you will start to make connections between places and people, wildlife and geological formations, and natural and cultural history. When the call of nature is answered, there is an integration of mindscape and landscape that will have lasting results.

Rattlesnake Point, Milton
NEIL HESTER

❑ Take a hike through the woods in the rain.
❑ Go for a winter walk right after a big snowstorm.
❑ Go for a wildflower hike on Mother's Day, when the flowers are at their peak.
❑ Go for a walk in the woods at night and try calling for great horned owls.
❑ Try chasing waterfalls at peak flows in mid April.
❑ Look and listen for frogs in a wetland at night.
❑ Go sideroading. Jump in your car and explore some backcountry roads. You'll be surprised at how much nature you can see from your car.

Walker's Line, Burlington
NEIL HESTER

❑ Photograph your family at the same natural site at different ages and during different seasons.
❑ Go antiquing — even if you are not looking for an antique. This is a great way to explore quiet backroads and see how pioneers were more connected to the land than we are today.
❑ Watch rock climbers scale the cliffs of Rattlesnake Point
❑ Go birdwatching during spring migration.
❑ Go steeple chasing. There are dozens of old churches in the Halton watershed. Their architecture and cemeteries are a testament to the hard-working pioneers.
❑ Make angels in the snow at least once during the winter. This is not just for children and don't worry about what the neighbours might think.
❑ Start a bird-feeding program. It's a fun way to have a regular dose of nature without leaving home. Be sure to put the feeder near a window where you often sit. You'll be surprised how contagious this pastime is. It's a great diversion from the monotony of daily living and an excellent way to learn about birds.
❑ Poke your head in a few crevice caves at Mount Nemo. You'll find that it's a different world in there and a refreshing thing to do.
❑ Walk the Trillium Trail at Bronte Creek Provincial Park in May. The rafts of white trilliums will amaze you.
❑ Go on a hike at Cootes Paradise marsh.
❑ Walk through Ontario's oldest-growth forest in any area on the Niagara Escarpment and imagine the prehistoric people who hunted in the same area and near the very same trees.
❑ Go on a snowshoe hike or a moonlit cross-country ski on Valentine's Day.

Cootes Paradise, Dundas
SUSAN HANSON

Hilton Falls, Milton.
RON KINDT

❏ Handfeed the chickadees in winter at the Hilton Falls Conservation Area.

❏ Go waterfowling at the Mountsberg Conservation Area. Seeing wild tundra swans during early spring is a natural sight to behold.

❏ Try mountain biking at Hilton Falls and, if you're really adventurous, the hills of Kelso.

❏ Explore the shores of Lake Ontario. Go for a hike on the Waterfront Trail.

❏ Take up golf. Yes, as much as some golfers might not admit, golfing is a great way to enjoy nature. In Halton dozens of golf courses include streams, ponds, valleys and escarpment cliffs.

❏ Go on a ruin ramble. Seek out old mills, chimneys and historic sites. They're educational and have a direct connection to nature.

❏ Go for a weekly walk on the boardwalk at Crawford Lake. It's therapeutic.

❏ Go skating on a farm pond. There's nothing like it, cracks and all.

❏ Look for animal tracks in the snow, and follow a red fox on his rounds in the woods.

❏ Rent a canoe or kayak and imagine a time when rivers were Halton's main transportation route.

Sixteen Mile Creek, Oakville
JANICE MCDERMOTT

❏ Join the Bruce Trail Club or buy a guidebook. You will be surprised at how many great hiking areas there are close to home.

❏ Go stargazing at night in the country. Seeing a falling star will get you through difficult times.

❏ Watch fish jump upstream at Lowville Park in April.

❏ Hunt for the elusive harbinger of spring, the eastern bluebird.

❏ Go for a paddleboat ride at the Kelso Conservation Area on Father's Day. Take your dad or your children.

❏ Take a horse-drawn sleigh through the woods at the Mountsberg Conservation Area.

❏ Visit the famous Royal Botanical Gardens during peak blooms of featured gardens.

❏ Visit the Iroquoian Village at Crawford Lake during each season and experience a way of life that had a direct link to the land, spiritually and for life's basic needs.

Sixteen Mile Creek, Oakville.
SUSAN HANSON

along the Beaver Dam Trail at the Hilton Falls Conservation Area.

❏ Build a treehouse in your backyard. Your children will love it, and it will be a wonderful source of childhood memories.

❏ Be a pooper snooper and learn how to identify animal droppings, or scats. You'll learn much about wildlife.

❏ Go on a scenic driving tour of Halton Hills. Stop at Limehouse and walk the Bruce Trail to view the ruins of massive lime kilns.

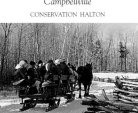

Gairloch Gardens, Oakville
MAGGIE MILLS

❏ Take up fishing. It is the greatest excuse in the world to enjoy nature.

❏ Try "pishing" in the woods. This is the sound birdwatchers make to attract birds in the wild. Birds are curious and often come to the sound.

❏ Put up a hummingbird feeder and watch these magnificent fliers put on a spectacular air show. The experience is uplifting.

❏ Explore the historic harbours of Bronte and Oakville and imagine a time when commercial sailing vessels made the harbours hum. These are great spots to daydream.

❏ Walk the Alexander Trail at Halton Region Museum and learn how this enterprising family generated electricity from an escarpment stream.

❏ Go on a scenic driving tour of Bronte Creek. You'll be amazed at the many natural treasures that can be found along the way.

❏ Experience the fall colour change at Halton conservation areas. It is particularly spectacular at Crawford Lake where colourful trees are reflected in the mirrorlike lake.

Mountsberg Conservation Area, Campbellville
CONSERVATION HALTON

❏ Go horseback riding in a natural area.

❏ Pick your own strawberries, apples or pumpkins and get your hands dirty while enjoying the great taste of the land.

❏ Make your own nature. Plant a butterfly and bird garden in your backyard.

❏ Search for the beaver house

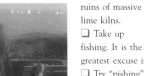

Halton Radial Railway Museum, Milton.
NEIL HESTER

Old is Beautiful Antiques, Moffat.
JACK ARNO

Kelso Conservation Are, Milton.
NEIL HESTER

❏ Try sailboarding at Kelso Conservation Area and feel the power of wind.

❏ Watch for bats in your neighbourhood, parks or open spaces that are surrounded by trees. Bats eat millions of mosquitoes during the summer.

❏ Take up cross-country skiing. It's never too late to learn this invigorating form of exercise, and it's a great way to experience the natural world in winter.

❏ Ride the rails at the Halton Radial Railway Museum in Milton.

❏ During autumn look for signs of animals preparing for winter.

❏ Visit a maple-sugar bush and taste the sap, or try maple taffy on the snow.

❏ Listen to jazz music on the grass slope of Oakville's Lakeside Park during the jazz festival in July. The Oakville Waterfront Festival, in June, has many venues along the waterfront, including Coronation Park.

❏ Go on a nature scavenger hunt. Look for acorns at Crawford Lake, along the Woodland Trail. The cap of an acorn makes a great natural whistle.

❏ Go for a hike with a tree-identification book and learn to recognize Carolinian tree species.

❏ Spend Thanksgiving at Crawford Lake and learn how the Iroquoians celebrated their relationship with nature.

❏ Take a hike and use a compass and natural landmarks to orient your direction.

❏ Plant native wildflowers in your garden.

❏ Participate in the interpretive programs at Halton's conservation areas. You'll learn much about Halton's natural and cultural history from park naturalists.

❏ Plant a tree on Earth Day, or start a recycling program at home as part of your own Earth Day celebrations.

❏ Feed the birds on Christmas Day. The people of Scandinavia traditionally spread birdseed on their doorsteps on Christmas morning to ensure good luck in the new year.

❏ Take up snowboarding and have a glide in the half pipe at Glen Eden Ski Area.

Mountsberg Conservation Area, Campbellville
GARY HUTTON

Glen Eden snowboard park, Milton.
SANDY BELL